Make Love to the Universe

HIMALAYAN MASTERS SHARE SPIRITUAL WISDOM

Make Love to the Universe

Phoenix Desmond

Wolf Trail Press
Eugene, Oregon

Wolf Trail Press
P.O. Box 10851
Eugene, Oregon 97440
www.wolftrailpress.com

The intent of the author(s) is to offer one of an infinite
number of interpretations of reality, which depending on your
perspective, may or may not be conducive to healing. The
author(s) and publisher disclaim any personal liability, directly
or indirectly, for any of the information presented in this book.

Editor: Elizabeth Smith
Book layout: William Morosi
Cover painting: *Make Love to the Universe* © 2011 by
   Benjamin Braun
Map by Benjamin Braun. Title set in Biographer.

Publisher's Cataloging-In-Publication Data

Desmond, Phoenix.
   Make love to the universe : Himalayan masters share
spiritual wisdom / Phoenix Desmond. -- 1st ed.

   p. : ill., map ; cm.

   ISBN: 978-0-9829159-6-7

   1. Sirius--Religious aspects. 2. Desmond, Phoenix--Travel.
3. Spiritual life. 4. Conduct of life--Religious aspects. 5.
Love--Religious aspects. 6. Nature conservation--Religious
aspects. 7. Concord--Religious aspects. 8. Esoteric astrology.
I. Title.

BL73.D48 A3 2011

133.9   2011920102

This book was printed on 100% post-consumer waste paper, processed chlorine free, using soy and vegetable oil-based inks. The cover was coated using an aqueous solution. To date, these printing methods have saved the following resources*:

10,454 pounds of wood: a total of 33 trees that supply enough oxygen for 16 people.
15,265 gallons of water: the equivalent of 888 eight-minute showers.
11 million BTUs of energy: enough to power the average American household for 42 days.
3,170 pounds of emissions: the amount of carbon sequestered by 37 tree seedlings grown for 10 years.
927 pounds of solid waste: the amount of trash thrown away by 201 people in a single day.

*Environmental impact estimates were made using the Environmental Defense Paper Calculator (www.papercalculator.org)

Acknowledgments

My heartfelt gratitude goes out to the following: the Sirian beings beyond all form and reason, who are the unofficial authors of this book; Suraj, for inspiring my wild adventures; the patient and persevering staff at Wolf Trail Press; Elizabeth Smith, my charismatic and thorough editor; Benjamin Braun, the remarkably talented artist whose painting graces the cover; William Morosi, for his outstanding design work; Craig, Jessica, Josue, and Stacy, for their early reviews; Fred Rogers at Aquarius Books, for his guidance and enthusiasm; my family, whose presence reflects powerful life lessons.

Last but not least, to Sandra, who has always been steadfast in her outpouring of support. Without her, I am certain that this dream would not have had the opportunity to merge with the human reality.

*To our allies in the spirit realm, for their
contributions to humanity's awakening.*

CONTENTS

Preface

It was the spring of 2007, and I was exploring the Himalayan region of India. Following in the footsteps of countless others before me, I had traveled to the East in search of a solution to the problem of the insatiable mind. Before long, the ancient art of yoga emerged from the depths of my being to reveal an answer. I became an initiate to its unfathomable wisdom, and our acquaintance quickly evolved into what would become a lasting friendship.

While lying in meditation one afternoon, I noticed a sound with a high frequency that I had never heard before. Although its pitch never changed, there was a quality to it that was calming. As soon as I sat up in bed, the sound seemed to disappear. Confused, I lay back down and turned on my side, with my ear against a shirt I had folded into a pillow. The sound returned, and was now noticeably louder. I arose from the bed and walked

outside to try and determine its origin. Except
for the chirps of birds in the distance, there were
no other sounds to be heard. When I returned
to my room, it dawned on me: the sound came
from within.

During meditations in the days that followed,
I learned how to tune my awareness to this internal
sound. I discovered that whenever I listened closely,
feelings of expansion and well-being would surface,
strengthening my sense of connection to all life.

Over the next few days, I noticed several
other internal sounds, each with a different
frequency. Some were high, while others were
very low. Some would enter my awareness for a
brief moment, only to leave without a trace. Three
became permanent—I learned how to tune to them
at any time of the day or night. Listening to these
particular sounds triggered a dramatic shift in my
awareness that opened my heart. Intrigued, I began
to search for clues that might somehow explain this
transformation.

Whereas my mind resisted any possibility
that lacked evidence, my heart brushed reason aside,
embracing the sounds as a miraculous and mysterious
gift. There was a brief skirmish between the two,
after which my heart eagerly moved forward with its
agenda of decoding the message behind the sounds.

Whenever I entered states of deep meditation, I noticed certain images accompanying them: light beings that were capable of taking any number of forms. Visions of the Sirian star system revealed their location. I watched the Sirians send their wisdom to Earth as vibrations with specific shapes and colors, which my heart interpreted in the form of feelings.

I have come to know the Sirians as my guides, since shortly after our introduction we united in spirit to embark on a journey that continues to this day. I realize that the mere mention of star beings will immediately raise a number of questions for many readers. Sirians are what we humans might consider to be a future version of ourselves. As such, they are not separate from us. They represent that part of our awareness that has overcome the problems we now face: fear and all of its consequences. The realm in which this awareness resides is invisible to most humans, for the simple reason that their present understanding of reality does not support its existence. This is understandable, especially when one considers that a unified awareness views all forms of separation as illusory.

In response to the inevitable cry of the skeptic, I will here emphasize that this book was not written with the intent of proving anything, but rather with the idea of offering an interpretation of the multifold reality we share. There is no logical explanation for the existence of my guides. The only evidence I can offer is the knowledge in my heart that the energies I associate with Sirians have brought me a considerable amount of peace during a phase of great strife on Mother Earth. My desire is to share the wisdom that I have gained by attuning to these energies, in the hope that it will benefit others in some way on their path of learning. I would expect nothing less than for readers to absorb only that which resonates with their innermost being, and discard the rest.

Since Sirians guided both my journey through the Himalayas and the writing of this book, the narrative that follows is told from the perspective of multiple speakers. While this may seem unusual at first glance, understand that it is both my intention, and that of the Sirians, to bridge the space of separation. We encourage all readers to abandon notions of indivi-duality and take their rightful place as participants in the story.

While unity is our ultimate destiny, it is also evident that the mind relies on separation to understand its reality. For this reason, "you" is used during spiritual discussions. This refers to humanity in general, rather than you as an individual. When we offer suggestions, know that we come from a place of love and equality.

On the human timeline, the story that you are about to read took place in the Himalayas of Uttaranchal, India, from April 23 to June 2, 2007. These details have no relevance to Sirians, since both time and space are constructs of the mind; step outside its confines, and you will at once realize that each detail of the journey is eternally unfolding from deep inside your heart. For this reason, the story is related in the present tense. Regarding its accuracy—as with everything you experience, that depends entirely on what you believe.

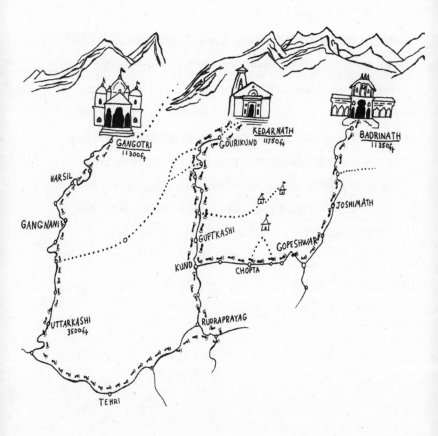

1

Arrival

*Nature is a living memory, of all that once was, all
that is, and all that remains to be. It is the gateway
between the source and its creation: the* we *concealed
within each* me. We *are the imagination of a Great
Spirit, a dream emerging from the darkness of the Great
Mystery.* Me *is an interpretation drawn out from
the dream. You are* me *asked to be made human. You
have chosen to come to Earth as part of your return
voyage to the source. Mother Earth is a pathway
Nature can take; she will nurture and teach you until
you ask to walk a different path. Wherever your
spirit may journey during your Earth walk, it is your
task to remember your connection to Great Spirit.*

arth began her life as a shared flame amidst
the hearts of stars. From deep within their
glowing spheres burned the impulse to extend the

breath of life throughout the canopy of space. Six stars came together for this, merging their light into a womb of fire that took the shape of their image. When they withdrew from their creative space, a scorching stone appeared in their wake. In joyful celebration they sang and danced. They encircled their beloved daughter from six directions, sending a strong wind in motion. It fanned the flames, cooling her body and setting her into place. Onto their newborn the stars projected their dreams, which descended in spheres made of water, fire, plant, stone, and air. They blessed her with the life-breath of their visions, entrusting her to follow their lead.

The task completed, Earth's parents chose a caretaker from amongst their numbers: a father to remain behind after the others had departed. He became both the guardian of her existence, and the navigator on her journey through space. His light would serve as the memory of life's origin, and the sponsor of its extension.

With the help of her father, Earth multiplied the spheres to create all aspects of land and sea, transforming her body from a bare stone to a lush paradise. Now Earth is overflowing with life. Her limbs are trees; her blood fills the oceans. Her voice is the entreating murmur of a wave at low tide, or the thunderous roar of a volcano at the moment of eruption. Her emotions are seasons, her thoughts the life-forms she nourishes. Her breath makes life possible for humans, as well as all other members of her tribe: the land walkers, the creepy crawlers, the green life, the water bodies, the stone people, the winged ones, the fire generation, the thunder beings, and the lightning clan. We thrive and subside alongside the beating of her heart. We worship and defile her, and she responds in kind.

Earth spins as she moves through space, sleeping and waking with a tilt and a wobble. Amongst celestial bodies are found her lovers, her most distant relatives, and her dearest friends. As she ages, her body changes shape and appearance, its land and water discovering new ways to meet. Her craters are battle scars, her mountains expressions of wisdom created to honor her ancestors. She can be playful or serious, cruel or forgiving. Her flaws are as numerous as her virtues, for after all, she is only a planet.

At the moment of our arrival on Earth, each of us becomes a member of her tribe, and every life-form we encounter becomes our relative. We agree to live in harmony with all of our relatives, meaning our actions encourage their well-being. To break this pact with our Mother is to oppose her Nature and become a fallen child. Whenever this pact is broken, one of two things will happen. The fallen child may remember the awareness that will restore harmony with Earth, choosing to stay with her tribe. A child that is unable to remember will remain opposed to harmony, and its spirit will be drawn into pathways apart from Earth.

Disharmony occurs while Earth is asleep. Whenever our Mother sleeps, we have to wait many lifetimes before she awakens. So each time before she falls asleep, she entrusts all of us to play her eyes and ears. If one of us falls, forgetting the agreement, our Mother asks that all children in harmony try to help the fallen child remember.

Earth has been in a deep slumber for centuries, and is just now beginning to awaken. The first thing our Mother will do when she wakes up is yawn and stretch. This will create a commotion; our homes will tremble, and a great wind will move in all directions. Then she will feel around her body for anything out of place. She will wiggle this way and that, using her Nature to restore harmony. Some land will sink under water, while some will rise to the surface. This is a wholesome event, and is necessary for the continuation of life on Earth. As long as we are in harmony with our Mother, we will move smoothly through these changes. We will experience a rebirth: an opportunity for all members of Earth's tribe to come together in love to celebrate our origins.

Humans are fallen children. You have forgotten your bond with your Mother, and are rebelling against her Nature. This is destroying, rather than preserving the rest of her tribe. Still, your Mother's love for you is so strong, that she has asked her distant relatives to help you return to harmony. In response to Earth's pleas, they have sent their children to join her tribe.

We are the children of a nearby group of stars known as Sirius, and have been allowed use of the body writing these words. Like your Mother, we want to see you flourish alongside your relatives once again. Although we cannot always be seen, we are using the language of the heart to transmit sound, color, and other sensations to you. Those who choose to act as open receivers first absorb our message, and then pass it on. An increasing number of humans possess the will to further our cause, opening their hearts to receive our message. We breathe through them for a time, directing their actions in the name of love.

Our intention is to offer humans the possibility of liberation from the illusion of separation. We will achieve this by revealing a human in pursuit of the Truth: the memory that love is the light that connects creation. Together we have chosen to undertake a journey, carried by our feet to serve our brothers and sisters on their path towards remembrance.

The Universe will protect and nourish this body that houses us on our voyage. If we radiate a compassionate vibration from our heart, its imprint will help fallen children to see the Truth, which will bring them back into harmony with Earth and her tribe. Some of our relatives will rise to support us on our journey, while others will stand in opposition to the Truth. We accept all interpretations as necessary. For even the stars would cease to shine, were we to remove them from the canopy of night.

We know you. You are fathers and mothers, brothers and sisters. We watched you from the light of the stars, stumbling beneath your chosen burden. The eye of the tempest has followed the path of least resistance, finding a resting place within your chest. Now the weight of separation presses upon your heart like the fierce wind of a tornado, filling you with dismay. The fall has left you confused, holding fast to solid ground. Crippled, you have turned from Earth's Nature, building walls to refuse entry. Do not resist her! She longs for your embrace.

You sense that the storm is passing. Emerge from your hibernation; allow us to show you a new dawn that lies in waiting outside your shelter.

2

Welcome to Eternity

Great Spirit is the self thrown into
the perfection of the present.

Himalaya: home of ice and snow. Spring has
arrived, and the snow has melted enough
to clear the roads. We have landed near the
headwaters of an ancient river. Great Spirit has
beckoned us to this sacred space using the language
of the heart. A swaying bridge rests under our feet.
Beneath us, to the east of the river, a solitary man
clothed in white garb appears against a backdrop of
solid stone. His hair is dark, and he has dark skin
and a long, dark beard. In an instant he is standing
beside us, smiling softly. He raises his head, peering
through spectacles. "Are you seeking a place
to stay?"

"Yes," we reply.

"What did you have in mind?"

"We are feeling it out, the land and its lay."

"Follow me, I have something that may interest you." The man in white disappears down a narrow path leading into the forest. Though small in stature, his movements are like streaks of lightning. As we follow, the town falls away behind boulders and evergreens. Reaching a small cowshed at the margins of civilization, we drop our bag onto a heap of tree limbs and pinecones.

"Why haven't you already unloaded all these things?" he asks. We glance at him knowingly, and step through the cowshed's double wooden door.

"My name is Suraj," he says.

Nice to see you again, old friend.

Suraj is everywhere at once. Lighting the wick of a corked flower vase filled with kerosene. Gathering pinecones from outside. Stowing them beneath a rusted metal cage resting atop a stone fire pit. Slowly, thoughtfully pouring water from an oil canister into an elderly kettle. The walls are made of mud plaster. The floor is dirt covered with a thin layer of straw and blankets. "Tried sand, it was too cool in the winter," Suraj says into the silence.

Our thoughts are few, our words fewer. Next to a bed of blankets, plastic bins rest against the wall.

They contain apples, ginger, milk powder, grains, and legumes. Buckets full of sugar. Suraj smirks mischievously. "Winter food rations."

Sweaters, hats, and backpacks hang on hooks overhead. Daylight struggles through a small, single-pane square window across from the entrance. Resting on the windowsill are prayer cards and beads, images of wise men, and withered flowers beside a ticking clock. Small bells hang above the window. He rings them. "A call to the present."

The sound penetrates our being, capturing our full attention. We suddenly sense the Universe to be contained within the walls of this room, with each sight revealing a world unto itself. There is nothing outside this moment. Wherever we exist, we serve as eternity's witness. We need only sit silently, patiently absorbing the unfolding present. While attending to the here and now, all suddenly becomes fullness. Here, where all space is sacred, and each secret whispers its answer.

Makeshift wooden shelves hang from the wall beside the fire. One supports a jar of homemade apple butter, tin cups, plates, pots, and pans. Another contains a row of amber vases filled with mysterious elixirs. Suraj is seated cross-legged, in *siddhasana.* He is stoking the fire with a metal rod, coaxing the flames with gusts of breath. The kettle is whistling. Suraj is squeezing lemons into tin cups, throwing in the peels. Adding bits of ginger, a heaping spoonful of sugar. Tea is ready.

3

Creation Is Alive!

Compassion is a fawn that treads lightly,
knowing all life to be sacred.

Suraj is a *sadhu*. *Baba*. Yogi. A wandering sage.
Though the words appear different, their
meaning is shared: a WoMan, male or female, young
or old, seeking unity in all aspects of life. He prefers
mountains to plains, being to doing, the lifestyle of
the hermit to that of the householder. Still, he likes
company—occasionally.

"One day I may go into town to eat at the
ashram (resting place), then I am okay not seeing
a soul for many weeks." He will sit by the fire for
hours drinking tea, listening without budging.

Suraj likes to walk. Every now and then
he will walk to distant temples. "Call me the

Himalayan marathon man," he says. He wrote a song about babas who travel by road, called "*Rasta Man.*" He will sit in front of the fire with a stick in one hand and a wooden spoon in the other, singing as he bangs on bowls, cups, pans—anything that will make noise. He used to have a band that played at restaurants and weddings. Suraj the rock star.

Suraj grew up learning about western music from travelers staying at his parents' hotel. Now he can sing almost anything, if you ask him: the Doors, Pink Floyd, the Beatles. He loves the Beatles. He even wrote a song for the girl he loved for her wedding day. He loved her so much that he wrote a song and gave her away. Babas have made a bad habit of giving too much away. Now Suraj is like Krishna without Radha, Buddha without Tara, Jesus without Mary Magdalene.

Outside, the sun is shining intensely. The Himalayas are a land of extremes: while the sun will warm you to the core, as soon as clouds appear, chilling winds begin their chase. We are traveling down a narrow and winding dirt trail along the riverside to visit the stone people. Here we can view them in every shape, size, and color.

Stone people are always leaping from mountaintops. Some land in the river and are washed

smooth. Others like to make piles. Every once in
a while they come together in just the right way
to make a home. Whenever we approach a stone
people's house, we have to first make sure that they
haven't lent it to another land walker. Just because
it's empty, doesn't mean it's open for business.
Sometimes the bear is off foraging for the day.
Other times the spirits are having a get-together. So
we must ask permission to be a guest. And since the
stone people are heavy and could fall and crush us, it
is wise to always ask before entering.

For every stone people's house, there are
many more land walkers, so babas build doors and
put locks on them to protect their homes. They
might use mud plaster to build an extra room in
front of the entrance. Some babas claim ownership,
renting them in exchange for food or money. It's a
long story, but at some point even babas forgot they
were only borrowing the stone people's houses.

Suraj is borrowing two stone people's houses,
one beside the other. One is big—three babas can
stand tall and not bump their heads. It has a fireplace
with pipes to direct smoke outside, and a canal dug
in the floor to remove water when summer rains
arrive. Suraj calls it a *shanti cutir*, a peaceful home.
Though he is fond of this home, he believes it is too
cold and wet to live in most of the year.

The other stone people's house is small, and
we have to crawl on our hands and knees to enter.
The stone people made it this way so that we have to
humble ourselves in their home. The leaks are sealed
with mud plaster, there are stone shelves for storing
food and wood, and the fireplace will heat the house
quickly. There is just enough space for a body of six
feet two inches to lie comfortably in the grooved dirt.
If we lay the body just the right way, the smooth,
round stone that protrudes slightly above the ground
fits neatly under the small of our back.

Suraj thinks this house is too small, but we
remember borrowing it many lifetimes ago. We
remember this because the house is inside a special
bubble of energy—a sphere that pulses slightly.
It is transparent, so we can walk right through it.
Whenever we approach the bubble, there is a very
slight attraction, like a whisper in our ear, or a tug
on our sleeve. The energy isn't always the same
color, but the feeling never changes. When we crawl
inside and listen with our heart, the memory returns.
Spirit is always communicating in this way; it is our
choice whether to listen.

We ask Suraj if we might borrow it again, to
rest our body for the night. Squinting and scratching
his head, he agrees.

4

Reclaim the Power Within

*Of your eyes, the two at the sides are for
sight. The one in between, for the vision to
remember that all you see is light.*

*Death is the appearance of all that is unseen.
To see with the eye in between removes
death from the dream.*

Light squeezes through cracks in the door of
the stone people's house. The sun is rising
over distant mountains, removing the shadow of
night from the valley below. Drowsy from slumber,
we throw off our blankets and open the door,
crawling into daylight.

Upstream, a man is standing on the opposite
side of the river. From a distance, he appears wild,

with dirt painting his face and tangles of hair growing in all directions. A tattered black robe clings to his body. The man is crying with arms raised, projecting his voice far across the valley with a high-pitched howl. These are no ordinary cries. He is wailing with such intensity that he is shaking from his head to his toes, his body drenched in sweat. An outsider to the human experience could listen to him and understand the full spectrum of emotion, from the pain of the deepest sorrow to the pleasure of the highest joy.

He is known as crying baba. Each day, several hours before dawn, he will walk to the river to cry. He does this again before dusk. He cries through thunder and lightning, rain and snow. He cries through thirst, hunger, and fatigue. He cries to hear the laughter of Great Spirit. For what begins as suffering must eventually meet its end in salvation.

Great Spirit can manifest as an infinite number of expressions. All activity of our body, mind, and spirit reveals our connection to Great Spirit. Crying, dancing—even an expression as simple as being—are all activities that radiate in waves from our body to interact with the Universe. Crying baba knows that when he wants to hear Great Spirit, he need only stand by the river and fill the valley with his song.

Farther down the river behind the temple, a flock of men, women, and children undress to bathe in the icy water at the river's edge. While they bathe, they submit their prayers to the river. They may pray for healing, for the well-being of family and friends, or for status and wealth. Some scatter ashes to honor departed spirits. Others fill bottles with water to use on special occasions. All of them are giving power to the river to answer prayers. This river is granted so much power that it is known to dissolve human bone in a matter of days.

※※※

If you wish to understand power, you must first understand the energy it is made of. Energy is light in motion. Light cannot create form without movement. Energy, therefore, is the essence of the physical realm. Power is the ability of energy to change form.

When a woman walks into a river of flowing energy with the intention of healing a dis-ease of her body, mind, or spirit, its energy will surround her being. The degree of healing she experiences depends on the belief behind her intention. If she believes in the power of the river to heal with all of her body, mind, and spirit, its energy will instantly transform her. If not, her form will remain unchanged. In both cases, her intention to heal will enter the river and take the shape of her belief.

The flowing energy of a river is no different from the energy contained within the human body. The only difference for the woman is where her beliefs place her power. Unlike crying baba, whose voice holds the power of transformation, she offers the power lying dormant within her to the river. The river in turn takes her power and gives it a life that she can see moving before her eyes.

❧

While tracing the footpath downstream on our way to the cowshed, we approach a line of mules walking in the opposite direction. The mane and tail of each mule is adorned with a different arrangement of bells and colored tassels. This seems to not only alert passersby of their presence, but also to help with identification.

The mules are wearing canvas packs with pouches hanging from both sides of their bodies, which are loaded with heavy stone people of various shapes and sizes. Their load causes them to stagger when they walk. A young boy follows closely beside each mule, carrying a long, canelike branch. The boys are making grunting noises and whipping the mules to direct them along the narrow trail.

Occasionally a mule loses its footing, tripping over stone people at the edge of the trail. This angers the children, who respond with a yell as they shove the mule and then whip it with more intensity.

Down by the river, several adolescent boys are striking stone people with pickaxes. Others shovel the fragments into canvas pouches while the mules stand and bear the burden. We recognize what appear to be the boys' fathers working in the distance, using the stone people to build walls along the road leading to the temple. We watch for many hours, absorbing the waves of suffering radiating from the mules. They appear fatigued against the heat of the midday sun, having been given no opportunity to graze or drink water since early morning.

Two mules stand gazing at the river, tied to heavy stones to prevent their escape. Undaunted, they are struggling to break free. As we approach them, they recoil from us in fear. When we offer them water, they forget their fear and drink with eagerness. A young boy approaches and makes a hissing noise, moving both hands in a sweeping gesture to drive us away.

Whenever a member of Earth's tribe creates suffering by exerting its will over another, it commits an act of tyranny. This severs the agreement with Earth to maintain harmony by respecting her tribe. The workers believe they must use force to build walls, and therefore have used their power to cause suffering for their land-walking relatives. They misuse their power because they do not understand the Truth of its endless supply. Were these men and children to realize the power moving through life, they would drop their axes and leave the mules to graze openly in the meadow. Like those before them in ancient Egypt, when many structures seemed to build themselves, they might simply try asking the stone people for help.

As Earth spirals through space, her tribe's awareness moves in a similar pattern. To understand this pattern, observe the spiral imprinted on the sole of your foot. Imagine that there is a line passing through the center of the spiral, and that one half is covered by shadow. The shaded half of the spiral is a symbol for the sleeping stage, while the visible portion represents wakefulness. While you walk along each ring of the spiral, you experience each stage of sleeping and waking.

The presence of tyranny is a sign that both Earth and her tribe have been sound asleep. When you first crossed the shadow of the spiral into twilight, you began your descent from a long day of light. Light is the Truth, the remembrance of our unity that harmonizes all of life. Your entrance into the shadow of night began with a nap. When the nap evolved into a slumber, you made your descent from the Truth. Now, after centuries of deep sleep, you have forgotten the Truth, and have fallen from harmony with Earth.

At the moment you read these words, the pitch darkness of night is making its way across the great divide and into the light. This event is known as the Return of the Golden Dawn. In your drowsiness, you may be only slightly aware of the current shift in awareness. As you again begin to trace the light half of the spiral, you will experience a gradual remembrance of the Truth that is empowering. What is now beginning as a flickering candle against a starless night will grow to encircle the darkness in a wave of light.

When your awareness crosses the great divide, the eye in the center of your skull will begin to awaken. Located between your eyes used for sight, it will only respond to the awareness of our connection. In moments of joy, when the feeling of connection returns to your heart, the eye between will open and begin to blink, sending electric sensations through your body. Blinking helps to remove cobwebs from your mind, which distort the Truth.

Once the cobwebs are cleared, the eye between acts as a channel for light to flow uninterrupted to your heart. This reactivates the ancient memory of the Truth. When this prophecy is fully realized, the light inside you will have grown to such intensity that no doubt of the Truth will remain in your mind. All words will dissolve before the feeling of light streaming through your body.

5

Still Your Mind

*All states of mind are chosen by the spirit
they walk alongside. If you wish to know the
activity of a mind, observe its surroundings.*

As we step out of daylight and through the
double wooden door of the cowshed, Suraj
hands us two tin buckets, signaling for us to fetch
water. Reversing our footsteps, we walk downhill to
the river below.

We hesitate upon reaching the water's edge,
startled by the amount of trash littering the shore.
Tin cans, foil wrappers, plastic bags — such are
humanity's contributions to the water bodies. To
think that anyone would so willingly desecrate such a
precious gift! Removing the trash from the river, we
walk to a spot where the water flows swiftly. Still, it

is murky from mudslides caused by quickly melting glaciers. The image reminds us of Suraj's words: "Such large glaciers aren't meant to melt so early in the spring." With so many members of Earth's tribe relying on glaciers for water, we wonder how long it will take for our relatives to listen to her pleas.

We fill the buckets, careful not to take up too much sand. Were we to drink the water without allowing the sediment to settle, the minerals would be so strong that they would trouble our stomach. So each time we collect water, we wait three days for it to settle. Then we boil it to cleanse it of harmful bacteria from pollution. We give thanks to the water before use, for allowing us the opportunity to live another day cradled in our Mother's arms. Whenever we remember to express our gratitude, the vibration we impart to the water cleanses both its body and its spirit.

When we return, Suraj is sitting patiently by the fire, having prepared two bowls of fruit. They contain sliced apple and banana sprinkled with bits of ginger. Such food is considered *sattvic* for sadhus, being simple yet nourishing. As he offers a bowl to us, he bows his head. "*Om namo nare.*"

This is one of many *mantras*, or phrases babas use to communicate a shared divinity. They believe that the more they repeat these mantras, the more power they have to transform our awareness from separate beings to a unified collective. While we eat, we silently reflect on the mantra.

The kettle is whistling. Suraj pours boiling water from the kettle into a tin cup, adding a spoonful of milk powder and stirring. He then reaches into a nearby sack and places a handful of oats into each bowl. Humming softly, he adds some warm milk. "Om namo nare."

Suraj is worried. The owners of the cowshed he inhabits say he owes rent for many months. They want him first to pay, and then part ways with his home. They plan to charge a higher rent to some men looking to house their cows. He frowns as he speaks, sending lines burrowing into his forehead.

Suraj has thought long and hard about this, and believes he has found a solution. He has inherited a large canvas tent with wooden poles. He wants to pitch the tent upstream, at the entrance to the shanti cutir.

Together we walk outside to the tent. After wrapping its canvas around the poles, we lift the poles atop our shoulders, heading down the narrow footpath leading to the cutir. The tent is heavy, so we stop to rest many times along the way. When we reach the cutir, we make a clearing and pitch the tent.

Suraj's brow is making lines again. He is worried about stone people falling and crushing him in his sleep. He looks around and notices that the firewood he has gathered next to his cutir is missing. While he paces back and forth, he rambles about the forest people: men wearing moustaches and green uniforms who sabotage sadhu homes. "Ever since one baba murdered another in his home, the forest people have been making trouble for us." We console him.

The next morning, Suraj decides that he wants to take down the tent and carry it closer to town, pitching it on some flat blocks of cement at the river's edge. We agree to help him, hoping to erase some lines. As soon as we finish pitching the tent, Suraj begins to gather his possessions from the cowshed and move them to his new home. Since he has limited space, he moves most of his food rations and kitchenware into the shanti cutir, leaving what's left in the cowshed. Feeling nostalgic toward his home of the past four years, he is reluctant to leave. "We will prepare our meals here until the end of the month," he says.

Poor Suraj, his mind is as scattered as his belongings.

Babas are everyday people. Even on the highest mountaintops, they will trouble themselves with the details of life. In fact, to spot a grown man or woman with an untangled mind is a sight as rare as a toothless alligator. Better to pass the day howling by the river with matted hair than to tie thoughts into knots that make a maze of our lives.

The mind is like a spider; its thoughts become the web it weaves. Spiders are masters of the art of weaving. They will focus all of their attention on completing one thread before weaving connections. Since they understand the structure of the webs they weave, they are able to connect threads without creating tangles. This enables them to always capture their meal with minimal effort.

An overactive mind will weave thoughts in all directions at once. Without the focus of the spider, it is always forgetting the task at hand. This results in a tangled web, and a frustrated mind whose work is never complete.

Like the spider, the mind must always understand its limits. It cannot travel in two directions at once, nor can it weave thoughts too close together. The web will be made stronger if all thoughts are connected. If the thoughts don't connect, they belong in a different web. The mind must have discernment in selecting thoughts for each web. A discerning mind is a clever spider that never strays from its web until the task is finished.

You can learn to untangle your mind through the practice of stillness. This practice begins with your spirit's intention. Spirit holds mastery over the mind. When your spirit wills your mind to be still, it obeys.

An activity as simple as fixing your attention on an aspect of Nature can help to create stillness of mind. For instance, sit in a grove of trees and watch their limbs waving in the breeze. Focus on the calming sound of rustling leaves. As you listen, you may notice thoughts begin to emerge. Each time you become aware of a thought, visualize it leaving your mind and being carried up and away by the movements of the trees. Allow it to dissolve into the atmosphere.

The more you listen to the trees, the less room you will have for your mind's activity. This will create a gap between thoughts. As the gap between thoughts increases, your awareness of their content and direction becomes greater. In this way, you can better separate thoughts that are productive from thoughts that are unnecessary.

Thoughts influence both the substance and quality of life. To hold uncertainty about future events is unnecessary activity for the mind; weaving future webs weakens the web of the present. When Suraj worries where he will live in the upcoming winter, he is unable to enjoy spring, summer, and fall. Weaving negative webs is also unnecessary, since they attract undesirable outcomes. Suraj would have more positive interactions with forest people, were he to believe that they are helpful instead of sinister. The clever spider never goes to bed on an empty stomach, leaving no doubts in her threads that would weave a faulty web.

6

Sit, Share, Listen

*Even the wise appear foolish before one
who brings peace to another.*

Exhausted from the labor of moving his belongings from the cowshed, Suraj is resting in his tent. Outside, swiftly moving clouds cloak the sun. The wind is behaving like a moody child that is unable to sit still, sweeping dust into our eyes. Wedging our body between boulders along the river's edge, we make our way into a wooded footpath leading back to town.

Terraced into the mountainside, cement walkways and bungalows gradually begin to replace the earthen floor of the forest. The bungalows face the river, and are painted in bright hues of yellow and red, with orange flags hanging above their entrances. In the distance, the clamor of pilgrims and merchants can be heard amidst ringing bells. The slow, baritone frequency of the forest fades to a low hum beneath the shrill urgency of the townspeople.

A young boy wearing a brown sweater and pants is sitting on a stone wall overlooking the river. When he hears us approaching, he turns, as if startled from a reverie. Surprised by our appearance, he quickly brings his hands together in front of his chest in a praying gesture, smiling and bowing his head. The revelation of love in this child is so strong as to greet even strangers as the dearest of friends.

We carefully cross the unsteady bridge above the river, gripping the ropes tightly while we tread its narrow planks. The stone walkway continues to trace the riverbank in both directions, lined with merchants selling sweaters, umbrellas, music, and precious stones. Young men stand in doorways, shouting to announce open rooms for paying guests. The smell of curry and the heaviness of fried food float through the air as restaurant owners dash about, enticing would-be customers to sit and eat.

To our right, crowds of pilgrims are passing under cement archways on their way to the temple. Many are carrying *prashad*: offerings of flowers, fruits, and sweets for their deities. To our left, babas dressed in varying shades of yellow and orange line both sides of the walkway. Some sit in siddhasana against the wall, others squat on their haunches, while a handful lean against pillars under restaurant canopies.

At the foot of each baba rests a small tin bucket with a handle, called a *kamandal*. Suraj once told us of its use. "The kamandal has different compartments — open the lid, and you will find a plate. Remove the plate, and there is a space for a cup. Kamandals are used to carry food and water while traveling. Babas will also use them when asking for *bhiksha*, or alms." Without the desire to gather wealth, babas often use monetary forms of bhiksha to buy *chai* and *bidis*, tea and cigarettes, for one another.

Babas are not beggars. Although they are considered poor by society, to a baba, wealth has nothing to do with possessions. They believe that prosperity is an ever-present reality that can be realized by committing one's life to understanding the Truth.

When an individual clings to the material realm, it forgets its impermanence. As soon as the fullness of creation begins to seem incomplete, the spirit falls into poverty. Babas therefore remain unattached to all that is material, and will share everything they have without giving it a second thought. Herein lies their power.

If you ever need to find a baba, walk to the nearest temple. Babas were visiting temple sites long before the towns and roads leading to them were conceived. Using their hearts' vibrations as a guide, they traced hidden trails to worship Earth's mighty monuments.

Nowadays, wandering babas hold council in the streets nearest the temple. Council consists of three activities: sitting, sharing, and listening. They sit because there isn't much use standing around unless you have somewhere to go. They share because they believe that everyone deserves to have abundance. They listen as a means of speaking without talking.

Babas understand that to listen is to honor one's relatives. Listening is an expression of love that strengthens our feeling of connection to the Universe. When we approach all life-forms as teachers, each interaction becomes an opportunity to learn by listening.

Amidst a group of elders sitting along the walkway to our left, a baba leans forward and motions with his hands in an open, sweeping gesture toward the stone wall next to him, patting htly. He is Nepalese, with narrow eyes, a thin, gray moustache, and a goatee. His figure is short and lean, with skin tanned like worn leather. He is sitting erect, with a strong demeanor. Like many of the babas, he is wearing layers of faded vests, ranging in color from red to orange to yellow. A thin orange cloth is wrapped around his legs and waist. It is knotted where the two ends meet, and is held in place by a thick and colorful embroidered belt. Another cloth is wrapped around his head. A light orange cloth bag containing some clothes and blankets is tied to a studded wooden cane resting at his side. The colors express his renunciation of the material realm in search of *moksha*: the liberation of a spirit from the cycle of birth and death.

Nepali baba removes his cane from the wall to make room for us to sit. We sit down next to him. With lips pursed, he lets out a wide, cheerful grin, scratching his goatee while he looks us up and down.

The surrounding babas huddle closer, seemingly amused by our appearance. After sitting in silence for some time, Nepali baba stands, as if he has reached a decision. With eyes opened wide, he tilts his head and raises his finger in the air, making his announcement to the crowd of babas: "*Hindustani* baba!" Pleased with his discovery, he repeats the phrase, which refers to us as if we are native to India. The laughter of surrounding babas carries a celebratory note that welcomes our return to their family. We join them, absorbing the warmth of their playfulness.

Nepali baba sits back down on the wall. Turning to face us, he lifts the index finger of his right hand to catch our attention. After pointing it toward the river, he opens his hand and raises it to the sky. Next, he folds his fingers into his palm as if grabbing hold of an item, and then gently rubs his hand up and down his opposite forearm. He switches hands, rubbing the other forearm. After again motioning to the river, he folds his arms in front of his chest, looking at us thoughtfully. Glancing at the river below, we spot a group of babas immersed in various bathing rituals. We smile, nodding our head. Nepali baba rocks back in laughter while he taps our knee.

A foreign visitor passes by on the streets. He appears young and of western descent. His bright yellow and orange baba garments resemble those being sold at a nearby merchant stand. He walks past us in haste on his way to the temple. After he passes, Nepali baba points his finger in the direction of the man. Shaking it back and forth in disapproval, he turns and points at us. He bows his head, folding his hands together in prayer in front of his chest.

Looking up, he raises his hands above his head with palms out, pausing for a moment. Then he joins his thumbs and forefingers together as if to accept a gift. Smiling, he taps his fingers on his chest and then lightly tugs his vest. He again bows his head and brings his hands into a praying gesture. We nod in understanding.

Nepali baba reaches into an embroidered bag and pulls out a small conical pipe made of clay, called a *chilam*. He removes several pinches of dried plant leaves from a pouch inside the bag, rubbing them in his palm with the fingers of his opposite hand. After carefully picking out the seeds, he passes them to surrounding babas to eat. A baba seated nearby unwraps a bidi and puts the tobacco into Nepali baba's open palm. Mixing the plant material together, Nepali baba grabs a pinch and begins to pack the chilam. When the chilam is full, he takes a small cloth from his bag and, connecting the thumb and first two fingers of his right hand, covers the base of the chilam with the cloth. With the bowl of the chilam pointing to the sky, he tilts his head slightly, cupping his left hand over his right while placing his mouth to the cloth.

A neighboring baba opens a matchbox, then removes a match and strikes it against the flint on the side of the box. After he raises the lit match to the open end of the chilam, Nepali baba forcefully inhales. When he exhales, he puffs rings of smoke out the side of his mouth, patting the fingers of his left hand against those of his right to gradually release the smoke. He then passes the chilam to matchbox baba. The chilam is passed from one baba to the next, until our turn arrives. As we take in the smoke of the sacred medicine plants, we feel respect for the wisdom they offer.

Babas believe there is much to learn from plants, since they have lived as members of Earth's tribe for much longer than humans. They spread their seed over Earth, blessing it with love. When the plants burst from seed with the advent of each spring, babas initiate a friendship with them. As the seasons pass, they encourage the plants to grow by singing praises for their beauty. When they harvest the plants from the wild each fall, babas give thanks for the plants' willingness to sacrifice their life-breath to nourish their relatives in body, mind, and spirit. This friendship is everlasting, fueled by the mutual love between babas and plants.

Babas understand that all green life carries medicine, meaning they have something positive to share. Their bark, leaves, flowers, stems, and roots take on the power given to them by the life-forms with which they interact. They can be eaten for nourishment, burned to strengthen prayers, made into salves and tonics to heal ailments, and even crafted into dwellings. All the green life has come to Earth's tribe to uplift their relatives, so that we may abandon our struggle amidst their splendor. They serve us in times of dis-ease, when we forget our ability to heal one another with the love from our hearts.

The clouds are lingering above us. A chilling gust spreads debris throughout the walkways. A younger baba approaches the group with flute in hand, clutching his shawl tightly. He is whistling a tune. Noticing our presence, he stops, surprised. Crouching in front of us, he brings his hand to his chest. "Baba Caneya."

We tilt our head and sweep our hands outward to introduce ourselves. He removes two small round beads from his cane, popping one into his mouth and offering us the other. We inspect the bead, bringing it to our mouth and cracking it between our teeth. It has a crunchy texture, and a peppery taste. Baba Caneya pats his stomach.

With a curious look, baba Caneya points to the wooden flute sticking out from our backpack. We remove the flute from our pack, lending it to him in exchange for his. It is noticeably shorter than ours, has fewer holes, and is made of a different type of wood. We play together for some time, sharing melodies and swapping flutes back and forth.

Suddenly, baba Caneya stops playing. Narrowing his eyes inquisitively, he motions with his hand to the shawl wrapped around his shoulders, and then gently places his hand on our chest. We shake our head in confusion. He begins rummaging through one of his bags, removing its contents. After pulling out a neatly folded white shawl with tasseled fringes, he allows one end to fall from the height of his shoulders. The shawl brushes lightly against the ground. It is made of fine wool, and appears unused. He offers it to us. We start to refuse, but he begins to insist. Suraj's advice surfaces in our head: *Whenever a baba offers you a gift, you should accept when you can, so you don't offend.*

We accept baba Caneya's shawl with gratitude. With the help of a nearby baba, he drapes it over our back and then shows us how to use our left arm to swing one end across our chest, so that it hangs from behind the opposite shoulder. As if by magic, the shawl instantly warms our body. Satisfied, baba Caneya wishes us well, disappearing amidst a group of passing babas. Still sitting silently beside us, Nepali baba points to the shawl, nodding in approval.

Seated on the opposite side of Nepali baba, an older baba with a scraggly beard and a moustache covering his mouth is observing our hiking boots with curiosity. He is wearing a worn-out pair of sandals, with many scars across his toes and ankles. Removing the boots from our feet, we offer them to him to try on in exchange for his. He removes his sandals and puts them on. They fit just fine, though he doesn't bother tying the laces. We stand to leave, wearing his sandals. He starts to take off the boots, but we put our hands up and gently push them forward. He cheerfully accepts our gift, and we continue down the walkway.

Farther from the temple, a baba with features resembling an ape is seated peacefully in the gap made between two adjacent walls. The whites of his eyes are clear, housing brilliant blue centers. He is gazing beyond the town into snow-capped peaks in the distance. Some nearby babas are making a game of tossing stone people against a wall. Others are singing and dancing to the music of baba Caneya's flute. A group of monks clad in yellow and maroon robes are browsing the music selection at a neighboring stand.

Peaceful baba seems almost invisible to passersby. We notice a pulsing sphere of golden light radiating from his heart. As the sphere pulses, it expands, containing first his body, and then those of surrounding monks and babas. It passes through our body, growing to envelop the town like a raindrop's ripples expanding in a lake. The energy sphere carries with it the feeling known by a newborn in a sound sleep. All of the babas hovering nearby peaceful baba appear to be basking in the vibration of the traveling wave.

A group of well-dressed western babas saunter past, their orange robes unstained by Earth's caress. Amused by peaceful baba's manner, they stop in their tracks. "Look at the glazed expression on his face—he appears to have gone mad! Who sits without stirring for so long, other than a drunkard?"

We lower our head, embarrassed by our brothers' accusations. If both a newborn and a sage are blissful, why praise one and yet ridicule the other? Peaceful baba remains in his trance, completely unaware of their cruelty. The western babas quickly lose interest, hurrying to the temple in search of a more dazzling spectacle.

The shadow of night creeps into the valley. After collecting our belongings, we wave good-bye to our companions and head back to the comforts of the cowshed.

7

Earth Is a Landing Pad for Spirit

Life is a school; our learning continues indefinitely.

We cross the threshold of the cowshed to behold Suraj, his back turned to us as he stirs the contents of a pot. Inside the pot is a soup containing chickpeas, potatoes, garlic, and green chilies. He half turns, acknowledges the shawl draped across our shoulders by tilting and then nodding his head, and resumes cooking. Taking our seat close behind him, we absorb the fire's offering.

While the soup simmers in the pot, Suraj removes some wheat flour from a stock barrel and throws it into a tin bowl, adding just enough water to make a stiff dough. With a spoon, he scrapes a small amount of amber sap from a jar. Mixing the sap in the bowl, he motions to the jar with his free hand. "A baba scraped this from the rocks across the river. Babas call it rock sweat, using it like salt for its many minerals."

Suraj kneads the dough between his hands, forming a round ball. Next, he removes a portion of dough from the ball and places it on the backside of a round tin plate. Using a tin cup as a rolling pin, he flattens the dough to take the shape of the plate. After making sure the dough is round and evenly pressed, he carefully removes it from the plate and places it on the metal grill over the fire. He watches it bake for several minutes, then flips it to the opposite side. Noticing our curiosity, he raises his head. "*Chapati.*"

The chapati is a staple in the sadhu diet; wandering babas are known to live on chapatis alone when other food is scarce. Babas waste nothing, learning to make use of what is available to them. Whenever food is offered, they make sure to take their fill. When they must go without food, they smoke green life, sing chants, and tell stories to forget their state of discomfort.

Suraj removes the lid of a pot containing rice from a nearby stone slab. After adding a handful of rice to each of two bowls, he pours the steaming soup to their brim. "Om namo nare." He bows while offering us the larger of the two bowls, uttering Sanskrit prayers in the direction of both the food and the fire. Removing a chapati from the top of the stack, he breaks it into pieces, tossing them into the darkness at a corner of the shed. "Offerings for the mice. They also have families to feed." A grin creeps across his face. "Besides, they make good companions. Unless you think a harmless creature scurrying across your lap is troublesome."

With a chuckle, Suraj wiggles his fingers, sliding his hand across his legs to mimic their movements. The innocence of his laughter reveals the tenderness of a modest hermit. To laugh often and without shame—such are the attributes of a flowering heart.

Our mouth begins to water as the soup's aroma awakens our senses. Suraj spreads a form of butter known as *ghee* onto a chapati, then folds it and dips it into the soup. Raising the chapati to his mouth, he pauses to glance at us. "Why so much interest in me? Eat, or your soup will soon be cold." We waste no time following his suggestion. After a long day with only chai and a chilam to mask our hunger, we appreciate the wholesome flavor of each morsel.

Suraj knows that we will be leaving soon— he recognizes the gleam of wanderlust in our eyes. We feel indebted to our brother for his loving service. By nourishing our body with food and the warmth of shelter, he has honored the spirits within. Such acts of kindness make him a wise teacher. His presence reminds us of our triumphs and pitfalls; the fears that create limitations along with the spirit of love that transcends them.

Suraj is an unknown sadhu. If you mention his name to the babas at the temple, they will shrug their shoulders and shake their heads. Like many before him, Suraj has renounced himself. He has sought refuge from the troubles of society in the Himalayas. Still, he wears a watch, pacing while he worries about paying the rent. He finds it easier to live in solitude than to open his heart to receive the love of another. And yet he croons love songs in his sleep. Like so many of us, Suraj tends to forget that by choosing to be a human, it became his Nature to love.

❧❧❧

Before its emergence from the Great Mystery, a spirit chooses a form based on its interpretation of the Truth: a robe that allows light to have a physical experience. The robe gives the spirit the freedom to interact with and learn from its relatives. The chosen robe will bring the spirit into harmony with a landing pad, which serves as a temporary home and school.

Mother Earth is one of a great number of landing pads for spirit. All members of Earth's tribe wear a robe, be they land walkers, creepy crawlers, green life, water bodies, stone people, winged ones, the fire generation, thunder beings, or the lightning clan. These robes are made of the spheres of air, fire, water, plant, and stone that descended to Earth at the moment of her creation. Upon arrival on Earth, the spirit takes up its robe, enrolling as a student in her school and beginning its education.

Mother Earth designs each experience to teach her students a lesson. At the end of each lesson, the student is tested. How it performs on the test determines the type of interactions it will encounter in the future. The student will know if it passes the test when it begins to encounter different lessons. Sometimes, even if a student passes a test, it may choose to retake it. This often helps to better remember the lesson. If the student fails the test, it will repeat the lesson by experiencing similar interactions.

On a spirit's journey through the many landing pads of existence, it will wear a great number of robes. Some robes will allow experiences in distant galaxies. Each time a spirit leaves a landing pad, it hangs its robe for others to wear. Spirit is continuously shifting between wearing the robe

of the physical experience and merging with the
formlessness of the Great Mystery.

Each day, you will make choices that affect
your experience as a human. The scenery and
characters of your story will always reflect the
lessons necessary for your spirit to fully rediscover
its Nature as an interpretation of light. Though
the outcome will be the same for all of us, your
experience on Earth will be forever novel and
mysterious.

❦

When we first met Suraj, we brought a
backpack containing many treasures from society,
such as money, books, and clothing. Many of these
objects now seem unnecessary for our journey.
Our state of abundance allows us to give freely of
all that we have, knowing that the treasure stored
in our heart will always provide. Sorting through
the backpack, we remove a shirt, a thin sweater, a
notebook and two pens, a small bottle of soap, a
camera, a tube of toothpaste, and a toothbrush. We
hand Suraj the backpack and its remaining items.
Wide-eyed with surprise, he silently accepts our gift.

Suraj springs to his feet, dashing to a nearby
food bin. "I have something for you as well."
Climbing the bin, he removes a sack from its hook

on the ceiling, handing it to us joyfully. "It is a baba bag—I made it from a jute sack used to store lentils." A green belt made of rope is stitched to the sack, serving as both a border and a shoulder sling. Inside the bag is an orange wool hat, a red comb with the inscription "BABA," and a long brown blanket. He shows us how to fold the blanket over our shoulder, resting the strap of the bag on top of the blanket to protect our skin from bruising. We wear our gift with pride.

The silence feels lonesome tonight, as if we have already parted ways. Suraj delays the sadness with stories: swarms of naga babas carrying swords and riding elephants on their way to the temple; tantric babas dressed in black, invoking the mysteries of magic; Aghora babas painted in white, summoning the spirits of their ancestors; female babas leaving their bodies unattended in caves to experience the lives of kings; ageless babas shifting between physical and spiritual realms; babas with wives and children; babas with only mountains as friends.

"Many babas speak of a man known as Master babaji," he tells us, "who is able to sit in meditation without moving, without taking food or drink, for forty days and nights. He is said to have lived in the same body for over three hundred years!

During this time he has stayed young and healthy, free from the illusion of time and space. Some say he can even travel thousands of miles in the span of a heartbeat to visit those who call him by name."

Suraj continues, "There are several babas who claim to have met Master babaji during their travels. They say he lives in the Himalayas, appearing to those who believe."

Spellbound by Suraj's words, we wonder if such a man could possibly exist on Earth. If so, wouldn't his presence prove our unlimited Nature? The possibilities excite our imagination; the hair rises on our arms as we consider what an interaction with Master babaji would be like. We express our interest to Suraj. "We would like to meet Master babaji!"

Suraj smiles.

Words give way to the fizzing sound of dying embers. We are seated on our ankles with knees together, face to face with Suraj. Candlelight sends his shadow streaking back and forth across the wall behind him. He closes his eyes, and his outline begins to blur. He is fading, his image merging with the darkness of his shadow. Suddenly, there is a faint whooshing sound, as though all the air in the room has slipped under the door. Suraj has disappeared. We smile and bow our head.

8

Transformation Begins with Intention

*Success happens whenever seeds are
sown with hope and excitement.*

reeping past rowdy restaurant owners, innkeepers, and merchants, we slip unnoticed through the gates at the town's entrance. At the outskirts of town, the neat arrangements of stone people beneath our feet once more give way to the earthen floor. Pilgrims on a day trip to the temple are filing in and out of an array of jeeps and buses lining the dirt road. As we walk farther from town, the melody of the wilderness begins to prevail over idle engines groaning in the distance.

The crunch of footsteps from one following close behind suddenly enters our awareness. Turning, we recognize the black garb and matted hair of crying baba. Without warning, he begins to bellow with laughter, waving with one hand while holding his stomach with the other. He stops abruptly, disappearing into the forest at the road's edge.

We continue walking. Though our legs are moving, the euphoric beauty of the landscape makes us feel as if we are floating. Whenever our awareness is absorbed in the beauty of Nature, all boundaries appear to fade away. Details grow hazy, and the much lighter currents of spirit replace the heaviness of our body.

Several paces ahead, a large bus is sitting slightly sideways at the edge of the road, its passengers standing in a large group nearby. Many are holding their heads in their hands, their body movements emitting anxious vibrations. We notice that the front wheel of the bus at the driver's side is leaning over the ledge of a treacherous cliff. The driver is crouching low, grabbing the front fender of the bus in an effort to try and lift it back onto the road.

A small group of men and women join the driver in his efforts to lift the wheel back onto the road. Shortly after they combine their strength, the wheel begins to budge slightly. When bystanders see the progress made, more join the group. The growing support strengthens their collective resolve. Suddenly, what began as an impossible feat now appears effortless, as the wheel slides back over the ledge and onto the road with ease.

※※※※※

All transformations follow the above pattern as they unfold. At conception, the idea to make a change may only hold the attention of an individual. As the idea evolves in the individual's heart and mind, an intention is formed. The intentions of the individual then submit a vibration to the Universe.

A vibration is a living extension of one's being; it travels like a boomerang that always returns to the thrower. When the vibration returns, it may take the form of beings, objects, and/or ideas to be used as tools to help fulfill the intention. The stronger the individual's belief, the more support it will receive. Whether a transformation occurs depends on the belief behind the intention. As long as the individual believes the intention will create a change, the Universe will continue to respond with supportive gestures.

Whenever the individual rejects a tool as unnecessary, the vibration behind the intention

changes. The Universe receives the request anew,
and then offers another supportive response. If the
individual begins to falter in its belief, the Universe
will put the request on hold until the doubt clears.
This dialogue between the Universe and its creation
is always changing, yet never ending.

❦

We continue walking, absorbing impressions
as they arrive. The distance is without measure,
the journey unrestricted by time. For Nature has
no time to think. Forever moving forward into the
present, our destination remains beneath our feet.

Daylight fades as the sun slips behind western
mountains. Peering through dusk's haze, we see
clusters of bungalows along the valley at the opposite
side of the river. In the distance, a uniformed man is
leaning in the doorway of a cement hut overlooking
the road. He has a blank, almost mechanical
expression on his face, his arms folded in front of his
chest in a defensive posture. When we draw near,
he exits the doorway and approaches. "Please show
your passport."

"We have none."

Our swift reply startles the guard, who is
now standing alert yet confused, as if shaken from
slumber. He clutches his chin with suspicion,

tapping his finger against his lips and narrowing his eyes. Unafraid, we smile broadly. After a long pause, he relaxes and lets out a sigh. He points at us knowingly. "Baba." The guard brushes his hands outward. We oblige, heading in the direction of a small town.

9

Fear Divides

When nations resort to arms, the human spirit is like a bird that cannot stand to hear its own song.

We cross a bridge at the town's entrance, admiring the sparkling river beneath our feet as it curves around a grassy grove of trees. A fence made of barbed wire wraps around the town's perimeter, defending its inhabitants from an unseen enemy. Near its gate, a crow rests atop the eaves of a vacant guard station, dutifully voicing the sounds of clicking heels. Cloaked by the crow's mysterious shadow, we pass through the open gate, following the road leading into town.

A handful of uniformed men with rifles slung over their shoulders are standing in a circle in the road. They are smoking bidis and talking casually beside a large green truck with a covered bed. Some of the men are carrying bundles strapped to their shoulders. They appear fatigued, as though they have been standing for much of the day. They squint at us through smoke clouds while we pass, glancing sideways at one another as if uncertain how to react.

At the center of town, a munitions stand, a barbershop, and a cafeteria stand at attention in front of rows of bunkhouses. A schoolhouse and a temple meet their gaze from the opposite end of the street, with a series of small bungalows peeking out from behind. The paint on each building is fresh, the walkways are swept, and the townspeople appear groomed and modest.

The sound of roosters clucking draws our attention to a nearby barnyard. A young woman with garments over her shoulder and clothespins in her mouth is stirring the contents of a large pot fired from below. Her downcast eyes and rigid frame discourage our approach. Many seemingly curious townspeople turn to ignore us with haste as we continue down the road.

At the town's limits, obstacle courses span the mountainside. A line of men are racing uphill, jumping through tires and swinging from ropes to the tune of a screaming whistle from a patrol tower high above. The cracks of rifles resound in the distance, as men fire at targets painted on bales of hay. The grunts and shouts of soldiers mingle with the familiar sounds of children at play; shielded by tree people, they sprint to and from the swings and slides of a small playground not far below the obstacle courses.

A trickle of curious adolescents emerges from the forest to hover near the courses, ignoring their siblings' pleas to participate in the games. They watch the soldiers with interest, awaiting the day they will join the ranks of men who are trained to fight for peace, in a war with origins nobody is asked to trace.

❦

War began one day as four brothers stood divided in a cornfield. It was the harvest moon, a time for all families to come together to share Nature's blessing. There was much to be grateful for, since this year's harvest was bountiful. Still, each brother had a wife and children, and secretly feared being unable to feed his family through the winter. When it came time for the brothers to claim an equal share, one of the younger brothers began to object. "How can we divide the harvest equally, when I have more children than the rest of you?"

As he spoke, a wave of anxiety passed over the group. Losing his patience, the next oldest brother raised his finger. "You may have more children, but my children are much older, and their needs are greater. If anyone is to get a larger share, it ought to be me."

The tension mounted as the two began to argue. All the while, the youngest brother stood silently listening in the background. When it became clear that the two brothers could not reach an agreement on their own, the eldest brother came forward to declare an alternative. "Each of us will reach down to the ground and take hold of a stone. We will then stand shoulder to shoulder and back to back, throwing the stones as far as the wind will carry them. Where they land, we will build houses for our families, facing the direction of the stones' throw. The land in front of each house, as far as the eye can see, will be that family's land, to do with as it pleases." All four brothers agreed to the proposal. They threw stones, building houses where they fell.

All was well, until one day, the youngest brother saw his uncle wandering the fields in front of his house. To help him understand the agreement, he walked from his door and began to build a fence where his eyes stopped seeing. Curious, the uncle called to his nephew from afar. "What is the purpose of this fence?"

"It is a line that divides what is mine from what is yours, to be sure that each of our families will have enough," the youngest brother replied.

"But this land was given freely to us by Earth. How can you claim the authority to divide our gift without first consulting your elders?"

"While we were busy harvesting, you were nowhere to be found! Besides," the youngest brother continued, "my family is larger than yours, and I need this land to grow enough food to feed my children."

The uncle, who happened to be a man with a heated temper, was not pleased with his nephew's answer. "Now you want to tell me where my family ends and yours begins! What is to stop me from removing this fence and reclaiming *your* land?"

The youngest brother's face became flushed with anger. "To step foot on this land is punishable by death." As he spoke, he reached down to the ground and lifted the same stone that had carried him from the shoulders of his brothers, hurling it in the direction of his uncle. The stone missed, falling in the dust.

Furious, his uncle confronted him. "From this day forward, I vow to fight for rights to the land you have claimed."

They began to quarrel daily, first throwing stones, and then forging swords to use against each other. Arguments became battles, and both men began to convince more and more relatives to choose sides. When it became clear that there would be no resolution without bloodshed, the youngest brother built a wall of solid stone in place of the fence. So meaningful was the wall to the brother—so fond was he of his creation—that he decided to give it a name: war.

Though the dispute with his uncle was far from resolved, the youngest brother was satisfied that his war would protect his family. Months passed, during which time neither spoke to the other. Then one day, the youngest brother saw his mother walking in the fields where his eyes could see. Upset upon hearing of her son's behavior, she had decided to visit him to try and persuade him to end his war. He rushed to her in desperation. "Mother, it is not safe for you here, you must return to your home!"

She laughed, scratching her head. "Not safe? Here you parade about, making speeches against your uncle, recruiting soldiers to fight for your cause. Tell me, to whom does your mother owe her loyalty, her son, or her brother?"

Her son stood speechless, embarrassed by her question. "Try as I might," his mother continued, "I cannot understand your reasons for division. How can I, when my heart pleads for a harmonious family?" As she searched for a solution to the conflict, she noticed a flock of birds in the sky, flying toward them. There were too many to count, flying with such grace that although they moved in unison, their wings never touched. She admired their movements as they wove over hillsides and in between trees. When they reached the mother, they formed a circle around her, dropping to her feet to feed.

She gazed at her son, who stood resolved behind his war. Pointing to the grazing birds, she said, "There will come a day when you will return to love, making peace with your brethren. On that day you will again seek me. Together we will tear down this wall that divides us." With that, she turned and disappeared into the tall grass.

※※※※※

Fear begins as the feeling of dis-ease within the heart. Walls are present wherever fear treads freely amongst humans. Building a wall to resolve a dispute is like covering a hole with a blanket; the feeling of safety it provides is illusory. Were walls to solve our conflicts, there would be no need for armies with weapons to defend them.

Were weapons capable of solving our
conflicts, there would be no need for warfare.
A weapon is an energy form forged by negative
emotions, such as hatred, anger, and greed. All
negative emotion is birthed by the dis-eased state
created by fear. To fire a weapon at a perceived
enemy is to consciously send a dis-eased vibration
out to the Universe. When we attempt to release
fear by directing it into our relatives, we extend it
deeper into our selves.

Were the brothers in the cornfield to remain
firmly bound by love, believing in the power of the
Universe to provide sustenance and foster well-being
within their family, their fear would vanish. In the
presence of cooperation, the complications created
by division are nonexistent. Whenever a united front
exists that is motivated by love, there is no challenge
the mind can pose that cannot be overcome.

❧

We sit to rest on a stone bench near a chai
stand. A group of men wearing blue jumpsuits
approaches, walking briskly. A tall young man
breaks from the pack, meandering over to the stand.
Noticing us seated on the bench, he begins to
question the vendor in Hindi, who merely raises his
palms and shrugs.

A look of intrigue flashes across the young man's face, and he again glances at us. He purchases a package of crackers from the vendor, offering them to us with encouragement. Our eyes light up at the day's first food offering. Excited by our joyful expression, the young man turns and purchases another package of crackers, handing them to us. Satisfied, he hurries down the road to catch up with his friends. His kindness sends a glimmer of hope shining forth from the gloominess of our surroundings.

A short man with a dignified walk approaches. He stops to sneer, standing over us and pointing his finger. "This is a military base." He searches for words, his chest swollen with pride. "We are responsible for the defense of our nation. Civilians are not allowed to roam the streets. You must pay for a room to stay in this town." Without the motivation to argue, we pick up our bag and begin walking out of town.

We cross the bridge as twilight announces its arrival. The road veers to the right, revealing a three-sided hut with a metal roof. The hut is vacant, most likely used to transport soldiers to and from the base throughout the day. After unfurling our blankets, we lie down to sleep.

10

Believe without Doubt

Trust is a butterfly emerging from its cocoon.

We awaken to the stillness of dawn, the faint rustling of a blue thrush immersed in its morning routine stirring us to our seat. The green life of the surrounding forest sparkles as the sun's filtered rays wipe away the dew of slumber. With a stretch and a yawn, we rise to our feet, folding our blanket in tune to Nature's casual rhythm.

Our legs begin to move without our mind's suggestion, destined south as they trace the road's gradual decline. The pounding of sandals against the ground quickens the blood flow through our body, reviving tender muscles. A line of cows traveling single file saunter by where the mountainside meets the road. They are followed by a herd of sheep

grazing in the pasture near the road's opposite edge.
As we absorb their tranquil vibrations, a small pack
of dogs surrounds us, barking furiously. Up ahead,
a pair of shepherds wielding canes scolds them, the
dogs reluctantly retreating.

In the distance, a young baba clothed in white
robes is hurrying up the road. His appearance is clean
and well kempt, with sparks of excitement emanating
from his eyes. Greeting us as he approaches, he stops
and begins to fish through the contents of his bag.

Giddy baba removes a colorful pamphlet,
opening it to show us its contents. Inside are many
pictures of an elderly man wearing white robes.
The man is seated on a throne carried by four men.
In each picture, his expression is serious, and his
posture is frail yet rigid. Alternating lines of red
and yellow are painted across his forehead, and he is
wearing a garland of multicolored flowers around his
neck. With his mouth open as though speaking, he
is pointing his finger in the direction of a crowd of
people gathered around him. Among the members
of the audience, none are smiling. The words *Kumbh
Mela* appear beneath one of the pictures, referring
to a festival where millions gather to celebrate their
relationship to one another.

Giddy baba points at each picture with
eagerness, talking rapidly and using the word

guru repeatedly. Guru refers to one who removes the darkness of ignorance. Many babas devote themselves to a guru, a teacher who instructs them on their spiritual path. We gather from giddy baba's gestures that the painted flower man is his guru, whom he is going to visit. He returns his pamphlet to his bag, salutes us with an open right palm, and continues on his way.

The image of the painted flower man haunts us while we walk down the road. He seemed solemn for such a joyous occasion, like a dark cloud about to burst. Those standing beneath his throne appeared to have been bracing for the type of downpour that accompanies the path of sorrow. How strange, for a happy baba to choose to devote himself to such a sad guru!

We cross a bridge leading into a village. As we approach the opposite side and sit down to rest, a man emerges from behind the door of a stark bungalow without windows. His face is stern and wrinkled. Noticing us, he frowns. "What is your business here?"

"We have none. We are resting."

"Babas in these parts are recognized by their special clothing, and their kamandals. You have neither. How can you expect to have food and shelter without these things?"

"The Universe provides for even the smallest of creatures, showing favor to none. We trust that the Universe will see to our needs as they arrive."

Flustered, he moves his hands in a familiar brushing motion. "Move on. This is not the place to beg."

We follow his lead, walking through the village. When doubt sneaks out from the darkness and takes the shape of a human, it is best to hear without listening. As we walk, we leave the doubt to wallow behind us.

At the edge of the village, a voice calls to us from the open doorway of a small, dimly lit bungalow. "Namaste, babaji! Come sit, have some tea."

The flames from a fire pit inside the bungalow illuminate a stout man with thick eyebrows and a round, animated face. We walk through its doorway and sit beside him on a bench near the fire. He begins to pour boiling water from a kettle into two tin cups. To one, he adds a spoonful of milk powder, sugar, and a pinch of black tea leaves, stirring before handing it to us. He then adds a heaping tablespoon each of milk powder and sugar to the other, stirring to make a cup of milk.

On the stove are two toasted pieces of bread. The man butters the bread with ghee, placing potato wedges from an oiled pan onto each half and combining them to make a sandwich. While we drink our tea, he eats the sandwich with his cup of milk. Though we are hungry, we thank him for his generosity and step outside. We feel confident that our meal will come soon.

We leave the village and begin climbing the mountainside. A nearby field of oats sways in the breeze, whispering an encouraging hymn. When we reach the top of the mountain, we sit atop a boulder to rest.

From our perch, we can see a great distance into the valley. To our right, the road winds through terraced fields of grain that poke out like stairs from a hillside. Several paces in front of us, the profile of a young boy's face appears from behind a nearby cliff; the rest of his figure steadily emerges as he hikes up an unseen footpath. When he reaches the top of the cliff, he begins to walk in our direction. With an apple in each hand, he playfully bobs his head back and forth. He is gently tossing the apples into the air, pleased by the smacking sounds they make when they land in his open palms.

When the boy approaches, he quickly glances from one hand to the next, and then extends his right arm to offer us one of the apples. We accept with gratitude, watching him begin to skip as he enters the fields behind us. While we eat the apple, we marvel at our Universe, lovingly engaged in play. For a moment, the ancient memory of paradise returns to our awareness.

We jump off the boulder and walk to the foot of the trail at the cliff's edge. The trail is steep and narrow, dropping between bungalows built into the mountainside. Although the road appears safer, veering off to the right and winding gently down the neighboring hillside, the trail traces a shortcut to the valley below.

As soon as we begin to descend the trail, we notice a two-story cement house directly to our right. The house is much larger than many we have seen, with numerous rooms and windows facing the open valley. A middle-aged man wearing a buttoned gold shirt and brown slacks is standing on the porch of the second floor, looking in our direction. When he sees us, he motions for us to come closer. We turn, stepping onto the cement platform in front of the house.

The gentleman looks at us inquisitively. Pressing his thumb to his fingers, he moves his hand to and from his mouth. We nod enthusiastically. With his finger in the air, he disappears into one of the rooms.

When he returns from the house, he motions to a nearby chair. We sit down on the chair, removing our bag from our shoulder. Behind us, an elderly man is seated in silence, casually observing us while leaning against a wooden cane. A young girl emerges from behind a closed door, bringing us a cup of water and a tin plate. From inside the house, we can hear the chatter of women and the banging of pans. While seated within the family's energy sphere, we feel a vibration that welcomes our presence.

Feeling at ease, we decide to say a prayer with our body by practicing a headstand. We fold a blanket and place it on top of the cement at our feet. After dropping to our hands and knees, we rest our forearms on the blanket in front of us and interlock our fingers, using them to cup the back of our head. Next, we raise our feet off the ground, lifting them straight up and balancing. The sensations created by standing on our head with the sky seated beneath Earth are refreshing. Many large condors circle us from high above, watching with curiosity. Birds of prey understand that all movements of the body are sacred, since they allow energy to take its various shapes.

The young girl returns from the house, this time carrying a tray with rice and beans. Our meal has arrived.

11

Speak with Your Heart

Love is a universal language; the
heart requires no translation.

fter thanking the family for the warm meal,
we begin to cautiously descend a steep, dry
creek bed. Near the valley, the bed reconnects
with the road. An older baba appears from the
underbrush at the road's edge, clothed in a jute sack.
He is barefoot, with silver hair and beard, turquoise
eyes, and bronze skin. After removing a bidi from
behind his ear, he lights it with a match and begins
to smoke. Though his lips are moving and he is
making sounds, we cannot tell if they are words.
He is gesturing grandly with his arms, reaching over
every now and again to kindly pat our shoulder. His
fatherly display is endearing.

With a wink and a smile, jute baba turns and begins to ascend the creek bed. We merge with the road and continue walking, all the while aware of a large tear in the strap of one of our sandals. Upon reaching a roaring waterfall, the strap breaks loose, the sandal falling off and sending us spinning into the dirt. We get up, remove the other sandal from our foot, and lay it beside its broken counterpart.

As we gaze at the crystal-clear water moving beside us, a transparent image of a fetus appears. The fetus is contained within a sphere of gently pulsing white light. Though submerged in the water, it is held in place near the waterfall's crest. Its arms and legs begin to unfold, its body spiraling as if leaving its mother's womb. It turns to face us, with flushed skin and dark, knowing eyes. They penetrate our heart, speaking in waves:

> *The body is a gift from Great Spirit, and is perfect in every aspect. When we emerge from the womb of the Great Mystery, we are without shoes and clothing. Since we are in harmony with the life around us, our bodies remain pure, covered only by skin. When the connection is forgotten, we depart from the innocence of the womb. Afraid and confused, we cover our bodies with layers that hide our true Nature. We believe*

that we must wear clothes to protect us and keep
us warm. And yet, none of our other relatives
have a need for such things. During the Return
of the Golden Dawn, humanity will again
harmonize with Earth, casting off all disguises.

The image fades into the background. When
we return to our body, the haze around us clears.
We continue walking. Now that we are barefoot, we
feel more connected to Earth, like a firmly rooted
tree. With each footstep, our feet send a bolt of
energy down to her core.

The road soon becomes rocky and
unforgiving. Our feet object to the sensations it
brings, like children rudely awakened from sleep. We
feel foolish to be uncomfortable in such a natural
state. A faint voice within encourages us to break
free from old habits of thinking that carry feelings
of pain. Our instincts take control, helping us to
avoid sharp stones by directing our attention to the
ground directly in front of us. The occasional patch
of grass at the road's edge relieves our discomfort.

While watching the vehicles pass by, we
wonder how their passengers are able to connect
with the beauty of the valley while separated from
it by moving walls. Just as we pose the question,
a large green truck approaches from behind. The

truck stops beside us, and a man wearing a beige
uniform rolls down his window and motions for us
to board the covered bed of the truck, from which
men can be heard conversing loudly. Recognizing
the man from the military base, we kindly refuse
his offer, shaking our head while motioning to our
feet. Surprised, he shrugs and continues driving. The
truck sputters away, its passengers waving from a
narrow opening in the back as it disappears around
the bend.

　　After the dust settles, we quickly regain our
momentum. The landscape before us is speckled
with stone people glittering in the late afternoon
sun. They smile from all directions, granting us safe
passage along their sacred road. A strong wind at our
back helps to carry us a great distance into the valley.

　　The sky above is splashed with crimson,
reminding us of the need to find shelter. Our heart
scans the river below, asking the stone people if they
have a house available for the night. We do this by
aligning our sight with the desire of our heart. At
first, the scenery grows dim as we broaden our focus,
ignoring the lines of our mind. Our heart then
emphasizes only those details that will help to fulfill
our need. It does this by interpreting the landscape
to guide our attention; details that appear to be the
most vibrant become signs in our search for shelter.

Suddenly, the road before us appears illumined against the dimness of our surroundings. The stone people seem to be encouraging us to forge deeper into the valley. We follow, leaving no room for our mind to interfere with their instructions.

❦

Each member of Earth's tribe has a voice that you can understand. If you wish to hear their message, you must learn to listen with your heart, rather than your ears. The heart understands that language consists of much more than simply words. The stronger your belief is that you share a connection with all of creation, the easier it will be for you to understand the voices of other life-forms. It is not enough for your mind to explain the connection. Strive to feel connected to the life that surrounds you, and you will begin to remember how to communicate with your relatives.

❦

Upon reaching a small hut at the foot of a bridge, we stop to rest beside its entrance. An older man is directing traffic from the opposite end of the bridge. Noticing our fatigue, he whistles to an idle truck farther up the road. After exchanging a few words with the driver, he motions for us to jump in the open bed. We approach the truck and, gripping a side rail, board its bed.

Many men, women, and children are descending a steep mountainside above us. Some have curious infants strapped to their backs, while others carry large logs cut from fallen trees. When they reach the truck, they heave the logs onto its bed and then climb aboard.

After everyone has boarded the truck, it begins to lurch forward over mounds of stone people, jostling logs and passengers alike. The movement is constant, but none are disturbed. Every so often the passengers call to the driver to stop the truck. As soon as it stops, more men, women, and children appear from the dense undergrowth of the forest to join the group. At each stop, all of the passengers shuffle closer together to make room. Though weary from labor, they cooperate like a large family. We feel blessed to witness a harmonious gathering where all are recognized.

The truck speeds deeper into the winding valley, its wide bed hiding the road beneath us. With the wind coursing through our hair, we feel weightless, as though flying. The peaceful vibrations of the family overpower the uncertainty of the truck ride.

The driver stops at a sleepy town whose streets slope uphill. Several passengers motion gently for us to get off. After jumping from the truck bed to the road, we wave good-bye to our relatives.

12

Love Unites

*The body is a temple. Each cell, a disciple. Its heart,
the altar. To enter the temple is to chant its sacred
Prayer. When the disciples are made to worship
an altar devoted to love, the Prayer illumines the
temple. When a temple becomes a luminary, disciples
from distant temples will draw near. When the
temple collapses, the Prayer fashions another.*

Near the center of town, we sit down and lean
against a tall stone wall at the edge of the
road. A fleet of buses arrives and parks in a line in
front of us. Several well-dressed men file out of one
of the buses nearby. They form a semicircle around
us, folding their arms and tapping their feet. After
several minutes, one of the men breaks the silence.
"Why are you sitting near the road?"

"We have been walking for much of the day, and our feet are sore."

He translates to the others, who nod to one another, speaking in affirmative tones. They begin digging through the pockets of their shirts and pants. Two of the men each hand us a bill for fifty rupees, and then they disappear with their companions into a nearby restaurant.

The clatter of coins against tin draws our attention upward to a baba seated on the wall high above us. We stand to address him, folding our hands and tucking them under our chin. He points up a steep stairwell.

Clouds of steam embrace us as we begin to climb the stairs. The clouds part at intervals, revealing glimpses of families bathing in pools of water to our left. Above us, earthen channels that descend from a flourishing forest guide the water into the pools. A small outdoor temple sits at the top of the stairwell, immersed in the docile vibration of the surrounding green life.

Our heart draws us to the spectacle of plant limbs sprawling in all directions at once, their emerald waves seeping into the temple's walls. A young *pujari*, or priest, is standing beneath the temple's canopy, leaning against a vine-covered pillar. When we reach its entrance, we notice what appear to be his wife and children seated at his feet. The family is dressed in luxuriant robes and jewelry. The pujari seems eager to welcome us into the temple, wasting no time as he begins to pose questions. "From which country?"

We answer politely.

"What is the occupation of your father, and what is his salary?" After a brief hesitation, we shake our head, refusing to answer. He is persistent. "At least you might tell me how many figures he makes?"

A nearby baba begins to chuckle. Blushing, the pujari rushes off to greet a group of visitors approaching the temple.

The woman remains silent, wearing a sour expression on her face. Beneath her lavish clothes and jewels and her smug expression, there exists a deep unhappiness, as if she would prefer to be somewhere else. To better understand her plight, we connect our heart to hers, receiving a vision of two families engaged in negotiation. They are discussing the fate of one family's daughter, who is seated at a distance from them, sullenly staring out the window. She is afraid and uncertain as the families sign an agreement involving an exchange of possessions.

The vision moves forward to a marriage ceremony. Throughout the ceremony, the bride and groom regard each other as strangers, as though meeting for the first time. The woman's predicament is clear: her family has made a decision for her to marry a man she does not love.

Having been forced into an uncomfortable situation by her family, the pujari's wife has chosen to feel unhappy. She is so overwhelmed by this feeling that she is trapped by the belief that there is no escape. Her heart is closed, her mind divided against herself. The key to her happiness lies in her heart, which she must trust to guide her to make positive changes in her life. Once she is able to open her heart in pursuit of the possibility of happiness, the door will open before her.

Rather than consoling the pujari's wife, we decide to allow her the experience of sorrow. After all, sadness is as acceptable an emotion as happiness. All states of being are equally meaningful, chosen by the spirit as lessons on its journey. The pujari's wife will return to happiness when her spirit is ready.

During your Earth walk, you will encounter relatives who repeatedly refuse happiness. If you actively try to persuade them to change, you will resist their natural course of learning. Your state of being is the strongest influence on others. If you wish for others to be happy, focus on achieving happiness within yourself, until the vibrations you carry become so strong that they inspire all who are touched by their waves. This will encourage the expansion of happiness into their hearts.

Happiness is conceived by love. To love is to be absorbed in the Truth of the unity of creation. Since love's pattern radiates throughout the Universe for eternity, it transcends all titles and material considerations. All members of Earth's tribe arrive and depart through this pattern.

Love is the feeling of warmth shared when two become one. This feeling awaits you at each moment, reaching out to your body and spirit. Whenever you foster unity in your interactions with your relatives, you are making love to the Universe. Like all states of being, your spirit must choose to feel unity; it can never be forced.

Being ever present, love is not taught, but rather remembered. The purity of your love depends on the degree of your realization of the Truth. When your heart is open to the Truth, it dances in love like a peacock in radiant majesty.

Union between any two life-forms is a sacred agreement that reflects a mutual love. When a man and woman are bound firmly by love, it will transform their lives, creating harmonious conditions through which abundance can flow naturally.

❦

We lie down to rest. Our feet are swollen, radiating sharp, painful spasms up our legs. Directly beneath us there is the sound of flowing water from an underground hot spring; its heat is passing through the marble floor of the temple and into our aching body. Drained from walking, we begin to fade into a different dream.

The sounds of approaching footsteps and voices stir us from our haze. With a flickering candle in his hand, the pujari emerges from the darkness, an elderly woman following close behind. She is carrying several plates of food on a tray. He offers us a small piece of white flesh from a coconut and then clears his throat. "You must meet my mother. She cooked a meal for you."

We squint our eyes in the candlelight, sending her a smile. After sitting up, we accept her offering, sharing the meal with two nearby babas. Feeling nourished and at ease, we lie down to sleep.

13

The Illusion of Possession

*Abundance is a kitten purring at your
feet, eagerly awaiting acceptance.*

Sunrise. Though the morning air is cold and moist, a short bath in the hot spring beside the temple feels rejuvenating. Soon after receiving the water's therapy, the pain in our feet seems a distant memory. We descend the stairwell to the street and continue south.

The road hugs the mountainside as we travel higher above the valley. Here many of the larger stone people lie sleeping beneath thick layers of sun-stained clay. Our footsteps echo far across the canyon to neighboring mountains.

The scenery quickly changes from a dense forest to a barren mountaintop. An eerie silence

takes the place of the sounds of wildlife, which
seems unusual, even at these heights. Our heart
speaks in alarming tones, alerting us to the deserted
landscape. We hear a mechanical grinding noise in
the distance, which is accompanied by ominous
dust clouds. Hesitant, we scan the mountainside
for an alternate passage, but its terrain is steep and
unforgiving. Ignoring our heart's warning, we decide
to move forward.

The sounds are becoming louder, the ground
beneath our feet now trembling. Suddenly, we hear
an explosion from the mountainside above us, and
a massive stone person begins to tumble in our
direction. It moves with tremendous speed, leaving
us vulnerable to its fury. An invisible force at our
back turns our shoulder to deflect the blow. As we
turn, the stone person collides with its relatives on
the mountain, bursting into smaller fragments that
fly in all directions. A large stone person grazes our
shoulder forcefully, plummeting into the river below
with a loud splash.

We let out a cry of pain and then crouch our
body impulsively. Dazed from the impact, we falter
near the cliff's edge. The invisible force returns to
raise us upright, encouraging us to keep our stride
by pushing from behind. Though weakened by the

blow, we stagger forward, trusting our companions in the spirit realm to lead us from danger.

Our strength slowly returns while we continue walking, astounded by the miraculous turn of events. In a few brief moments, a force as subtle as the wind spared our body from death; a spirit with the insight to sense the danger ahead, and the willingness to guide us to safety. To think that many would consider spirits frightful, perhaps even demonic! When humans perform such courageous acts, they become celebrated heroes. Consider the possibility that spirits exist to serve as guardians, concerned only with our well-being while we explore Mother Earth's landing pad. Are spirits invisible by their Nature, or have we simply chosen not to see them?

We approach a man-made stone people's house reaching far into the mountainside. A group of miners caked in dust emerges from its mouth. They are pushing a wheeled cannon with long metal spears loaded in its barrel. Inside, several miners wearing helmets and wielding pickaxes are aggressively striking stone people. Still others are gathering large bundles of precious gems in their arms. We sigh upon discovering the invaders, who have entered Earth's womb to loot her treasures.

Stopping to rest at a nearby chai stand, we pull up our sleeve to inspect the wound. A surrounding group of miners gasps at the sight. Although our shoulder is bruised and bleeding, the cuts are shallow, and are already beginning to form a scab. We are relieved by its appearance, feeling grateful to have been spared from the stone people's wrath. Several of the miners seem puzzled by our reaction. If they knew of our narrow escape, they might have reserved their gasps for Nature's infinite power.

❦

The heart is the seat of power. All activities that bring joy to the heart allow the seeker to realize its power. This power is invisible, like the wind. It is the foundation for all worlds, bringing with it the ability to accomplish any feat, or answer any need. When the heart is immersed in love, each experience is complete as it unfolds.

If your heart strays from love, it is because you refuse to accept the reality that you are already complete. You may feel dissatisfied with your circumstances, causing you to forget your heart's power to bring fulfillment. The inner conflict thus created leads you to the material realm for answers. Changes in your perception of Nature may cause you to manipulate your relatives in attempt to resolve your unhappiness. Manipulation can take many forms, such as reducing a winged one's feathers to mere objects of trade, or viewing a rolling meadow as a piece of land to be used for personal gain. When you consciously surround yourself with material objects, you fall into the illusion of possession.

To create personal gain at the expense of one's relatives is to forget that abundance is ever present. What right does any member of Earth's tribe have to lay claim to its relatives? If you disregard the life present in even the smallest stone, you have committed a disservice to both Earth and her tribe.

Your body was crafted from the elements beneath your feet. All that is material will by its Nature fall away, returning to the elements from whence it came. If you clutch firmly to the most impermanent aspect of your self, you will gain nothing more than dust and vapor. On the other hand, whenever your activities follow your heart's commitment to harmony, you grow closer to understanding the prosperity of spirit that endures forever. Make love your highest pursuit; know it to be eternal, its power beyond measure.

We enter a small town. The streets are empty, save a yellow-bellied bird perched atop a thornbush. The brilliant image of the bird stands out against the starkness of the town, inviting us to take a closer look. Entranced by her beauty, beams of love travel from our eyes into the object of our adoration. She tilts her head in reception, her gaze penetrating our being. Chirping sympathetically as though moved by our hunger, she hops to a nearby bush. The bush is speckled with clusters of bright orange berries. She opens her beak slightly, plucking a berry from the bush and swallowing it with ease. With a joyful whistle, she darts into a nearby thicket.

We approach the bush and begin foraging for berries. Though small, they are tender and juicy, with a sweet citrus flavor. Gathering handfuls with eagerness, we absorb the nourishing vibrations as the juice tickles our throat. We silently thank our friend, and then continue into town.

Up ahead, two elderly men are sitting on a stone bench near a chai stand. One of the men is smoking a bidi, staring listlessly into the cobblestone street. Both men are wrapped in several blankets, with small bundles of clothes at their feet. We reach into our bag, remove the money given to us in the temple town, and divide it between them. Wary of our gesture, one of the men collects his belongings and disappears into a nearby alley. The other begins to snicker, rushing across the street to a chai stand and snarling to scatter some of the customers. We shrug, unattached to their response. After all, the feeling of joy brought by giving should never depend on the reaction of the recipient.

We survey the hillside, noticing the familiar sight of terraced grainfields; a sign of the rugged and resourceful attitude that prevails amongst those who dwell in the Himalayas. After climbing the green staircase, we find a comfortable tuft of grass on which to lie down. A solitary bird sits nearby, singing melodiously. While we meditate on its hymn, all thoughts begin to dissolve. There is a sensation of expansion in our head, as though a door has opened. A soothing voice reassures us as we surrender our body and step into the unknown.

14

Competition

Listen closely to the Law of One.
Know it to be without exception.

he first rays of sunlight are streaking across neighboring fields. Following their ambition, we fold our shawl and blanket and then toss them over our shoulder, strolling through the countryside in search of the road. A glimpse of a car speeding past helps us to chart our course amidst waist-high grass. After reaching the road, we continue south.

In the distance, a family is picnicking under a giant oak tree beside a car parked by the roadside. A young boy and girl eat thoughtfully, while the father and mother beckon to us. After approaching and crossing the road, we sit across from them on a lavender wool blanket. "We saw you walking three days ago on our way to the temple," the mother says. "Now we are driving home, and here you are again!"

The children begin to laugh, and their mother opens a woven picnic basket and sets out its contents with eagerness. There is fried bread and sweet rice with curried peas and peanuts, along with many sugary confections of various shapes and colors. As she offers them to us, waves of compassion radiate from her energy sphere. Although the food is sweet and heavy, we eat ravenously, remembering our hunger from last night.

Almost instantly after finishing, we feel bloated and dizzy, like a child visiting a circus who has had too much candy. Astounded by our hunger, the mother offers us an extra bundle of bread for our journey, which we accept. As the family gets into the car, the young boy offers us his chocolate bar. We hold up our hands in refusal, and then lightly pat his shoulder. His gesture feels more filling than all the food in our stomach.

Moments after the family drives off, a bus stops beside us, its driver offering us a ride. We board the bus and find an empty seat, and he continues driving. The bus rolls indifferently over large stone people in the road, with each bump traveling through the seat and then up our spine. After a brief ride, we arrive at the outskirts of a large town.

The weather has changed noticeably, the clouds above squinting their eyes in the retreating sunlight to release a halfhearted sprinkle. After exiting the bus, we find temporary shelter beneath a stone arch, which stands at the front gate of a large white ashram. The ashram has several floors, with many more rooms arranged in rows. Long verandas with marble pillars and walkways protect the entrances to the rooms, which face a river at the opposite side of the street.

Many babas wearing pristine robes of white, yellow, and orange stand along the walkways, looking out at the river. They appear restless. Upon noticing us, they break their silence and begin talking. Some point in our direction.

A baba with a shaved head approaches us and opens the gate to lead us to the others. An elderly gentleman wearing tan slacks and a checkered brown and gray sweater emerges from the group. "How can I help you today?"

"We could use some shelter from the falling rain."

"In order to stay here, you must be under the instruction of the resident guru." There is finality in his tone. The other babas begin pleading with him in Hindi. A brief argument ensues. Frustrated, the gentleman throws up his hands and hurries upstairs.

Our concern fades into relief as we observe the friendliness of the remaining babas, who are satisfied with their victory.

A young, charismatic baba with white robes and neatly combed dark hair approaches, his brothers following at his heels. He points to our feet with curiosity, looking at us as if awaiting an explanation. We point to the straps on his sandals, connect our thumb to our fingers, and then quickly pull them apart. After a few attempts, charismatic baba begins to nod in understanding, turning and disappearing into a nearby room.

He returns promptly with a small box. After opening the box, he removes a pair of blue sandals. The sandals are made of rubber, each with two diagonal straps meeting between the first and second toe. He offers them to us, urging us to try them on. We slip them onto our feet, wedging the thick rubber strap between our toes. Although the rubber feels uncomfortable, the sandals fit nicely.

A middle-aged baba with narrow lips and a pointed nose emerges from the shadows, dispersing the group of babas with a disgusted look. He marches forward with confidence, his large frame and grave manner possessing an intensity that seems to lunge ahead of his body. His features are as sharp as his movements, relieved somewhat by curly black tufts of hair bouncing wildly atop his head. He halts in front of us, breathing heavily as though disturbed. Leaning in close, he inspects us through slitted eyes. "For weeks before your arrival, the babas of this ashram have followed my instructions to practice silent reflection. In their meditations, they have journeyed far into the depths of wisdom. A foreigner stumbles past the gates, and suddenly they throw themselves into a frenzy!"

Hoping to alleviate the severity, we say, "They must have found wisdom to be boring, to have been distracted so easily!"

Inflamed, guru baba continues, "A ragged man such as yourself, without so much as a destination is a poor excuse for a baba. You are lost, a wandering fool in need of guidance. Why behave like an animal, always struggling to find food and shelter? Only under the supervision of a guru will you learn the discipline and responsibility necessary to reach enlightenment. If you join our ashram and agree by its rules, you will study ancient scriptures and practices that many men before you have used to attain *Samadhi* (spiritual liberation). When you complete your training, you will be given papers to prove your achievements as a sadhu. These papers will allow you to enter many ashrams, temples, and residences where you will be offered food and lodging. One day you may even find yourself in a position of power, advising others on their path toward Samadhi." He scans his surroundings, seemingly in search of support from the group of babas lingering nearby. The babas follow his cue, nodding while they mumble approvingly.

We reflect on his words, tapping our finger to pursed lips. Although we disagree with guru baba, it was never our intention to disrupt the order of the ashram. Then again, what fault is there in offering one's opinion, even at the risk of condemnation? Set ablaze by our deviance, our thoughts follow their impulse to form words. "Brother, look around you. The babas of this ashram are restless because they are deprived of the opportunity to embrace their humanity. Humans learn wisdom by simply living according to their Nature. All life-forms are spiritual, regardless of how they choose to behave. Would you think a wolf is foolish to roam the countryside in search of its meal?"

"No, but wolves are wild animals," guru baba says. "They do not possess spiritual knowledge."

"With our limited perspective as humans, how can we pretend to understand a wolf's relationship to creation? We may be ignoring wise teachers by perceiving our animal relatives as ignorant beasts."

Steadfast in his beliefs, guru baba continues, "The babas at this ashram are working toward a higher realization, something you do not seem able to understand at this time. Perhaps one day, after experiencing much suffering while wandering through society, you will change your mind. When you are ready, our ashram will welcome you." Satisfied, he turns and walks briskly down the veranda, his sandals tapping like clockwork against the polished marble.

⁂

In his quest for illumination, guru baba has become competitive, assigning rules and limitations to the most defining feature of existence. The Truth is that light streams from every pore of your body, connecting you to your relatives in Earth's tribe and beyond. Spirituality is your essence! There is no price to pay, no routine to follow, no guru necessary to recognize the light that courses through creation. Each movement is a revelation of divinity, regarded by Great Spirit to be neither wrong nor right. You are sacred as is, your existence stretched along an infinite string. None are denied access to this holy reality. Only your mind can resist the Truth. This realization is true liberation.

When you are competitive with your relatives, it is as if you are looking down into a pond from above, and yet unable to see your mirror image. As soon as you believe that you are greater than your reflection, your mind finds reason for division. Ask the birds of the flock why they cannot exist apart. "We are stronger, wiser, happier as one," will be their unanimous response.

Hierarchies are both imagined and held in place by patterns of mind. Your mind disguises the Truth behind the veil of separation. Use your will to remove the veil, in remembrance of the guru that is everywhere at once. When you are able to erase the boundaries of your mind in favor of the Truth, hierarchy will be replaced by the vision of equality.

The time has come for humanity to bow in reverence before creation, like a devotee singing praises to its guru. Embrace your relatives like a mother would her beloved son, so that we may again stand united to witness the Return of the Golden Dawn.

❀❀❀

A bell chimes, and the babas disappear into their rooms. A door opens to reveal charismatic baba, blushing with embarrassment. He quickly glances back and forth down the walkway and then encourages us to step inside. After we enter his room, he leads us to a bed covered with a fresh pair of sheets. Beside the bed, a warm glass of milk rests on a nightstand. We drink the milk and lie down to sleep, our eyelids surrendering to gravity.

15

The Great Mystery

Acceptance brings peace. Its wisdom is compassion.

ising before dawn, we gather our belongings
and hurry outside, passing through the gate of
the ashram.

The street is a mud puddle etched between
dwellings stacked on top of one another. The rains
have subsided; trailing winds weave between bed
sheets and blankets draped over balcony fences
above. As we squeeze between rows of fruit and
vegetable stands at either side of the street, farmers
swat flies with rolled newspapers to protect precious
produce. A small herd of cows lingers nearby,
awaiting the opportunity to seize a snack at the first
sign of distraction.

Farther from town, the gradual return of green life begins to subdue the bustle of the marketplace. The straps on our sandals rub awkwardly against our toes, which show early signs of blisters. While we remove the sandals from our feet, a group of babas approaches. One of the babas is barefoot. Preferring to be at Earth's mercy, we offer them to him. He frowns, apparently sharing our opinion. Upon seeing his response, his companions plead with him as they point up the mountain to the journey ahead. Embarrassed, he accepts our sandals, and the group continues into town.

We approach a wide bend in the road with a large truck parked at its edge. A baba emerges from the darkness above the hatch of the truck's covered bed. He is plump and cheerful. With wide-eyed enthusiasm, he brings both hands to his chest to summon us into the bed of the truck. Quickening our pace, we toss him our bag and grab his outreached arm, climbing over the hatch of the bed.

After we crawl inside, two more babas become visible, sitting on planks of wood. They bow to greet us when we sit down across from them. One is a young man with warm brown eyes, glossy beard and hair, and a full-toothed smile. His expression is pleasant and innocent, his eyes shining as he offers us a handful of crackers. The other is

much older, with a frail, stern manner. Whenever
we smile at him, he softens his gaze, offering us a
glimpse into the friendly child hiding beneath.

A muffled conversation enters the bed from
outside near the front of the truck. A door to the
cab closes. The engine wheezes while the truck
starts, and the floor of the bed begins to tremble.
Plump baba slides a plank of wood in our direction.
We place it under our seat, bracing for the bumpy
ride ahead.

The truck moves forward, and the mountains
begin to retreat from the opening above its hatch.
Before long, their sharp peaks are replaced by
the warm air and rolling hills of lower elevations.
Unprepared for the dramatic change of scenery,
we feel a hint of sadness to be leaving the tallest
mountains behind.

The truck quivers as a wheel beneath us
strikes a stone person, sending us rolling across the
metal floor into the opposite corner of the bed.
Plump baba dashes to our rescue, grunting while
lifting us to our feet and then slowly leading us back
to our seat.

Hoping to avoid injury, we begin to watch
our brothers' approaches to the sudden lurches of
the truck. Stern baba firmly grabs the floor and
walls, drawing his body erect like a threatened

rooster. His movements seem to create more tension than they resolve. Pleasant baba bows his head and brings his knees to his chest, folding his arms across his legs like a turtle drawn into its shell. When we mimic his defensive posture, we feel trapped in a state of hopelessness. Plump baba lies on his back on a wooden plank. He interlaces his fingers and then rests them on his chest, drifting peacefully off to sleep. He appears as weightless as a jellyfish, the walls and floor around him a rolling ocean of energy. This posture looks the most comfortable, being the least resistant.

 When you became a member of Earth's tribe, you chose to take a ride with your relatives. Our Mother has offered her body as a playground for all of us to travel across during our ride. Each member of Earth's tribe will have a different experience that depends on the robe it chooses to wear. For instance, an eagle will witness life on Earth much differently than a whale.

 If you were without your body, you would be able to see from every angle at once. Since you can only witness a small part of existence in your current body, there is much that remains hidden. We call this unknowable aspect of life the Great

Mystery. Embrace the Great Mystery, and you will experience a state of balance that puts you at ease with your surroundings. Reject the Great Mystery, and your experience becomes a struggle for control that conflicts with creation.

Balance is like a frog in a pond that leaps from one lily pad to the next without faltering. Because it breathes steadily through each experience, it moves effortlessly in tune with Nature. Expect sudden bumps along the way, and you will have made the first step toward achieving balance. Know that plans will be thwarted, maps redrawn, and the path will go on without end. Do not feel threatened by this. Learn to be as flexible as a jellyfish, until you can breathe calmly amidst uncertainty. Emerge from your shell; understand that by accepting the Great Mystery, you allow magic to enter each experience.

The truck slows to a stop. Grabbing our bag and swinging our legs over the hatch of the bed, we jump down to the dirt road. Our friends do the same, wasting no time as they begin to walk swiftly downhill. Rather than trying to keep their pace, we walk gently, attentive to the soreness at the soles of our feet. From a distance, they remind us of a marching line of ants.

Near a cliff at the edge of the road, two men are leaning against a shiny motorcycle, enjoying the panoramic view. They wave to greet us. "Would you like a ride?" one of the men asks. He proudly lifts his chest. "I am the policeman of this town. This is my apprentice, who I am training. It is our responsibility to help travelers. Do not worry." The apprentice nods enthusiastically.

The idea of a plainclothes policeman driving without a helmet is foreign to us. Besides, how can three people fit on one motorcycle? Still, his tone and gestures reveal that his heart is open, and his intentions are pure. The peaceful image of plump baba resting comfortably on the plank returns to us. We accept his offer, getting on the back of the motorcycle.

The policeman continues, "I am teaching my friend here how to drive a motorcycle. We are going to coast downhill to the station. It is eleven kilometers from here." We laugh nervously as the young apprentice raises the kickstand and pushes off.

The road is narrow and without lanes, the cliff to one side dropping off treacherously. The apprentice winds around the mountainside, honking to alert oncoming traffic before each bend. The landscape blurs, and we surrender to the unknown, waving to plump, pleasant, and stern baba as the motorcycle speeds past them. The policeman turns his head sideways. "You see, it is easy! Would you like to give it a try?"

We laugh, shaking our head. "No thank you, we are only here for the ride."

16
Judgment

Seek fault in others, and you will discover an endless stream. Embrace all life as perfect, until faults become distinctions to be set free. And though the divided mind will sketch lines and choose sides, the heart holds the colors to fill the spaces left behind.

The motorcycle slows to a stop at a solitary bungalow at the base of a steep mountain. The policeman turns to us. "Here is our station."

Dismounting from the motorcycle, we glance uphill in anticipation of the climb. "They are building a new road leading to town," he continues, "which is only a few kilometers from here. Good luck on your journey." He opens the door of the station, disappearing into its dark interior behind his apprentice.

A few paces ahead, the sharp debris of stone people arranged into a trail replaces the road—the apparent aftermath of the adjacent mountainside's demolition. We slowly, carefully make our way uphill, scanning the ground directly ahead of us in search of the least painful route. Despite our efforts, the jagged terrain cuts the soles of our feet, which begin to leave behind a visible trail of blood. Fears surface as the midday sun pours into our body without mercy.

A lizard is lying motionless in the shadow of a stone person. The lizard appears to be dreaming, its eyes blinking rapidly as its tongue flits in and out to relay a message: *Slow down. The possibilities are infinite.*

We sit by the roadside, contemplating how to transform our awareness of pain. If we fail to change our awareness, we risk being unable to continue walking. Though the mind is known to hold firmly to familiar patterns, we know that the heart can empower the spirit to change them. Our challenge is to change the pattern to prevent serious injury.

Suraj once told us a story about fire walkers: babas who choose to walk across scorching stone people. He described how fire walkers quiet their minds to make a painful experience comfortable. We follow their method, focusing on steady breathing while walking. With each successive breath, our awareness withdraws further from the tension. Sensations of pain lessen as the flow of blood from the bottom of our feet stops; their skin begins to mold to the contours of the stone people.

Our mind suddenly awakens, continuing its conversation with a handful of tall buildings looming in the distance. The sight of a forgiving layer of fresh asphalt at our feet brings relief.

Upon reaching town, we sit to rest on a bench shaded by a metal roof. A vendor approaches, wheeling a cart. "Where are you traveling to?"

"As high as our feet will carry us."

"Do you have a place to stay for the night?"

"This bench will do just fine."

He chuckles. Overhearing us, a nearby man joins the conversation. "Are you sure you want to sleep on a bench, when there is a temple right behind it?" We turn to see the white walls and bronze steeples of a large temple, its arched windows surrounded by a golden fringe. The man playfully taps the vendor on the shoulder. "Why don't you give him one?"

With an irritated expression, the vendor slides open a door at the top of the cart and then buries his arm inside. He pulls out an ice cream cone, afterwards reluctantly handing it to us. His friend says, "Go on—eat it before it melts!"

Even the vendor smiles at this. We follow the two men to the stairwell beneath the entrance of the temple, licking the ice cream before it can drip down our fingers. The joker walks up the stairs and opens the double wooden door of the temple, calling to someone as he steps inside. Moments later, he returns with the pujari, holding his arm while he brings him down the stairs.

The pujari greets us with a quick bow. "There is a room at the back of the temple for you to sleep. But first, wash your feet at the faucet near the door. My wife and I will cook a meal for you." The three men lead us to the entrance of the room at the back of the temple. They remain behind to chat while we wash our feet and then step inside.

The room is large and empty, with enough space for dozens of babas to sleep comfortably. Near the window, the whirring sounds of the ice cream cart enter from outside. We lie down to rest, dozing in and out of one after another realm of spirit.

Back at the temple, the door of the room begins to creak open. The vendor, joker, and pujari enter, accompanied by another man. The pujari is carrying a tray of food, which he places in front of us. A procession of shy young children trails behind.

All of the men approach and bow, sitting around us in a semicircle. The children linger nearby with downcast eyes.

The joker lets out a whistle and then grins. "I would like you to meet my friend. He is a fellow teacher at the English primary school. These children are our students. Some are also our sons and daughters." The teacher and children bow politely. He continues, "We brought them here to learn from you. You see, we think that men and women of your skin color are privileged, since you were born into wealthy families. We want to know why you have come here without even a pair of sandals for your feet."

"Love is without such considerations. The purpose of our journey is to fully awaken to the realization of love, for the benefit of all of our relatives."

The vendor raises an eyebrow. "To give to others is wise, but give too much, and a man will meet his demise. How can you take care of yourself without money?"

"By knowing that in Truth, the Universe will always answer our needs, given that we believe. We give what we are able, all the while taking what we need. In the same way, we must empty our lungs, to fill them once more."

"But what will you eat?" he asks. "And where will you sleep?"

"Can you not see this feast that you have placed before us, or the roof above that shelters us from the cold? To live from the heart is to throw the worries of the mind to the wind. If we aren't concerned that the wind will provide us with the breath of life, why should we bother with such details?"

Unconvinced, the vendor continues, "Wandering from place to place may work for you, but what about men and women with families to take care of? How can we expect to have a home or feed one another if we choose play over work?"

"Life is a game," we say. "Think of yourself as a child at play, free to choose the game and its rules. If you want a warm home and wholesome food, how would you like to obtain them? You can work all day, half the day, or not at all. Do you think the work ought to be difficult and miserable, or simple and pleasurable? When you work, should you be standing or in motion, or can you be sitting or lying down? Do you have to grow food to eat it, or can you buy it from the market? If you offer encouragement to the farmer, aren't you working by helping with *his* work? If you sat patiently for long enough, might food fall from the sky? Ask yourself these questions. Use the answers to form your own interpretation of the Truth. Above all, take responsibility for the rules of your game. If you are unhappy with the outcome, have the courage to change the game!"

The vendor shrugs his shoulders, folds his arms, and raises his chin, staring past us into the corner of the room. He is thinking hard, struggling with a set of beliefs that challenges his own. The joker breaks the silence. "You are much like a young Buddha without his begging bowl!" All the men begin to laugh.

The vendor regains his confidence, shaking his head in disbelief. "A fool relies on the charity of others. Take some responsibility — you cannot expect your needs to be met by invisible powers!"

We sigh as we watch the children hovering near their teachers, absorbing our conversation. "Each of us has the responsibility to choose the beliefs that shape our experience. Whichever beliefs you choose, know that Buddha is a potential that lies within all of us. Look to your children to remind you of a Truth that will never escape you."

The vendor stands up, turns, and walks out of the room.

A limitation is a thought that has concealed everything outside its view. Judgments are limitations that obscure the Truth. The heart isn't capable of judgment. It can only absorb impressions, responding with a feeling. This creates a vibration in the body, which travels upward to the mind. The mind behaves like an intricate artist, interpreting the vibration by painting a canvas.

At birth, the canvas of your mind is blank. Your heart speaks without words, and life is a seamless transition from one experience to the next. Each moment after birth is an opportunity to witness the wonder of Nature. You are an actor in a play with a mysterious plot, one in which you are blessed to have been given a part. Like an artist with your experience as your canvas, your thoughts and feelings will paint lines, shapes, and colors to fill in each detail. Your expressions, in turn, become the brushstrokes for Nature's evolving masterpiece.

If you give your mind leadership over the magical language of your heart, it will organize each experience into a thought. Thoughts that are repeated will eventually become judgments that fill your canvas. Since the brushstrokes are repeated, the artwork ceases to change. Likewise the play loses its mystery, as the actors, scenery, and even the ending remain the same.

Children are clever artists: they paint a picture one moment, and then throw the canvas away. In this way, their art never repeats the same theme. They will paint a lightning storm, and then replace it with sunshine and rainbows. Or they may fall from a tree, only to land in a pile of leaves. For when the heart is absorbed in the magic of play, the mind will approach its art as an ever-changing game.

⁂

Muffled laughter vibrates through the walls from outside, and the remaining men notice the absence of their children. Bored from the adults' endless play of words, they snuck outside to gather sticks and tin cans, organizing a game of cricket in the alley. We stand by the window in between the pujari and the joker, watching the children intently. From within their magical realm, each moment appears to be filled with the joys of a simple and spontaneous game.

Our brothers snap from their daze, remembering their role as fathers. They look to their watches, yawning as they return to their minds' scheduled programs. Time to feel tired, to corral the children and prepare the family for bed. Tomorrow will be a busy day.

17

You Are Unlimited

*Great Spirit sings one Truth. Existence is its
presentation. The presentation divides into bodies of
vibrations. Vibrations impress upon one another, like
raindrops meeting in a lake. What we give and what
we take becomes the pattern behind our shape.*

Morning. A young woman with lush eyelashes
who is wearing a garland of flowers draped
around her neck enters the room carrying a silver
tray. "You must take some food before you leave. It
will give you strength for your journey."

After removing our blanket and sitting up, we
rub our eyes and inspect the contents of the tray. A
cup of chai sits next to a stack of chapatis smothered
in ghee. Beside them is a plate containing a banana,
a mango, and a pomegranate. The woman places the

tray on the floor and stands to leave. "When you have finished, wait for the pujari. He will take you to my father's house." She turns, stepping through the open doorway and into the street.

We follow her advice, lifting a chapati from the tray and biting into it with a loud crunch. It tastes rich, sinking unpleasantly into our stomach. Putting it aside, we peel the banana, chewing delicately in between sips of chai.

The pujari enters the room hastily, bringing his fingers to his mouth with encouragement. We pat our stomach and squint our eyes. "*Khatm, dhanyavad.*" (Finished, thank you.)

He shrugs, then wraps the chapatis and fruit in a napkin and hands the bundle to us. "Stow this in your bag. You will need it later."

We walk outside beside him, following the dirt road leading to town. He pauses near a group of bungalows neatly lining the street, cupping his hands over his mouth as he calls to one of the residents inside. A door opens, revealing the soft-spoken teacher from last night. The teacher approaches and winks at us, burying his hands in his pockets. "Namaste, babaji. After listening to your story last night, I wanted to help you. Is there a place you want to visit, or a person you would like to see?"

"We are seeking a man who lives in the Himalayas," we say. "He is known as Master babaji."

The teacher scratches his head. "Ah, Master babaji. I have heard of him, but haven't met him. They say he travels like the wind. If that is true, then he could be anywhere!" After a brief hesitation, he continues, "Masters live in the tallest mountains of the Himalayas, where they can watch over the people. If you want, I can send you thirty kilometers north by bus. It isn't far, but it will help you to avoid the heat of the foothills." He glances at the scars on our feet. "Can I offer you a pair of sandals, to protect your feet? The road ahead is rocky."

Noticing the absence of shoes in the doorway, we realize that our friend is offering us his only pair. We shake our head. "No, thank you."

The pujari sighs. "As you wish. If you ever pass through this town again, you are welcome to stay at our temple." He bows, turning and disappearing into a crowd of people.

The teacher leads us to a nearby chai stand, purchasing a ticket and handing it to us. A bus approaches not long afterward, rolling to a stop in front of the stand. We board the bus and sit by the window. A young boy walks down the aisle, tipping his hat to greet us and then stamping our ticket.

We wave to the pujari as the bus sputters off, braking frequently on its way down a dangerously steep road. After a few kilometers, it stops again, and many men, women, and children board and exit. Empty seats fill quickly with passengers; more remain standing, crammed in the aisles.

As soon as the bus pulls away from the stop, a burst of hot air tickles the nape of our neck. We turn to see a young man with beads of sweat on his forehead, panting and grinning widely. He perks up in his seat. "Hey, weren't you outside at that ashram, chatting with all of those babas a couple days ago?" As he speaks, plump, pleasant, and stern baba become visible, walking in a line outside. We laugh, nodding. Babas share a kinship of heart, and cannot help but crowd together.

There is a light tap at our shoulder. We turn to see the ticket collector. "This is your stop . . ."

Outside, the sun is at its zenith, and a transparent haze is writhing upward from the street's pavement. The hot, dry air of a lazy marketplace surrounds us. Vendors and townspeople slouch under the sparse cover of shade trees dotting the sidewalk at both sides of the street. The soles of our feet quickly begin to burn with intensity. Hopping from one foot to the other, we make our way to the sidewalk.

While passing through the crowd, a group of restaurant owners begin to close in on us. We rub our thumb and fingers together, opening our palms and shaking our head. "*Nahin paise.*" (No money.) They quickly comprehend our gestures, turning to approach nearby visitors. Relieved, we continue north, away from the marketplace.

The town transitions into a wide plateau resting in the space between steep mountaintops. We walk several kilometers across a rocky and barren terrain with the sun shining overhead. Once-familiar green life is now a distant memory, in a land without the comforts of shade. The road is vacant, save the occasional vehicle stirring up dust clouds as it roars past.

The sun lowers his glare to signal late afternoon. Still, the heat remains. With parched throat and tender feet, we consider heading back to town. Despite being unable to find any signs of water, we are warned by a voice from within: *Keep moving—do not be still.* Our vision blurs, and images begin to repeat.

Exhaustion slows our pace, leaving us vulnerable to negativity. Resentment swells from within—at the sun, the mountains, and the apathy of passing vehicles. The more we dwell on our situation, the worse we feel. Stranded in an unforgiving landscape, our hope grows dim.

The consequence of each thought and action now seems more immediate. Negative thoughts swirl around us, imprisoning our body in a state of dis-ease. Recognizing their influence, our heart intervenes, helping us to focus on the removal of suffering. We accept the circumstances and surrender to the uncertainty of the outcome. Acceptance is our ally, for it has the power to catapult us from the depths of suffering into more pleasant states of being.

Thoughts of the pujari remind us of the bundle of food in our bag. After opening the bundle, we peel the fruit and eat it ravenously, saving the chapatis for last. We reach deeper into the bag, discovering a forgotten pair of socks. Although they are thin and full of holes, they offer a layer of protection from the burning pavement. The improvements rekindle hope. Positive thoughts replace negativity, our vision becoming more lucid as a dilemma turns into an opportunity.

A cloud crystallizes from the clear blue sky, hovering between our body and the sun to shield us from its rays. Empowered by the miracle of Nature before us, we quicken our pace. The sounds of trickling water emerge from a nearby granite cliff. Steady droplets of water are falling from one of several small round holes on its surface. Ecstatic with our discovery, we hurry to the hole and cup our hands to catch its blessing. A small pool of water forms in our hands. We drink the water before it can seep through our fingers, licking them to capture every drop.

Our thirst quenched, we walk with confidence across the plateau. At the edge of a bend in the road, the plateau drops off into a valley harboring a wide river. We find a safe path to the river and begin to make our descent, passing between large boulders. Upon reaching a sandy beach, we toss our bag near the shore and undress, walking into a shallow pool of water at the river's edge.

Before long, the frigid water's energy restores our strength. Satisfied, we get out of the water and find a comfortable place to lie on the beach. As the sun dries our skin, we reflect on the movements of energy between the sun, the river, and our body.

Spirit basks in a cosmic field of energy. When your spirit chooses to take up a robe, it continues to have full access to this unlimited source of energy. As your mind develops, it grows into an awareness that sets limits for your body. For instance, your mind will tell your body when and how much to eat and drink, when to rest, and how long to sleep. These limits are both created and maintained by patterns of mind, and can change at any time.

All states of being involve a transfer of energy, with spirit both giving to and taking from the Universe. Think of your body as you would a vehicle, with its energy contained within a fuel tank. When the fuel is spent from activity, your body must refill its tank. To eat a bowl of rice is to absorb an amount of energy determined by your mind to nourish your body. A bite from an apple could satisfy your appetite as much as a bowl of rice, if your mind were to believe that the two contain the same amount of energy.

For Master babaji, the energy contained within his breath supplies his body with all of its needs. He has transcended the awareness held by most humans that nourishment depends on eating food. Since he remembers his unlimited Nature, his tank is always full. This enables him to go without food or drink, rest or sleep, for as long as he pleases.

Love opens your mind to the possibility of overcoming limitation. It does this by first shattering patterns of mind that divide and give rank to energy forms, and then encouraging those that create unity through equality. The more you are able to open your heart to unity, the more energy will be available to strengthen your body, mind, and spirit.

The state of fear, on the other hand, encourages the creation of limitations. A mind consumed by fear is like a king huddled behind the walls of his castle, brooding in the darkness of its innermost chamber. Just as light cannot enter a closed casket, energy cannot penetrate a body in refusal.

Negative thinking supports limitations created by fear. When we held resentment toward the sun for its heat, our emotions depleted our stores of energy. The division created limited our awareness to a suffering self, and thirst and fatigue began to drain us. When we again chose to open our heart to our unlimited Nature, each experience became an opportunity to replenish energy. Holding firmly to love would have helped us to avoid states of suffering altogether.

✦✦✦✦

We stand up, dressing and then gathering our belongings. The soft pink and orange hues of sunset encourage a state of ease as we scale the cliff leading back to the road. Peaceful sentiments outlast the lingering doubt in our energy sphere. It is now clear to us that the energy we spent while suffering was not in vain; positive and negative states of being have equal value on the path of learning. Besides, how can one waste an unlimited supply?

18
Release Blocked Energy

Suffering is resistance to a presentation of the Truth.
Happiness is deliverance from suffering.
First accept.
Now let go.

Thoughts of food and shelter resurface amidst the stillness of twilight as fireflies blink to the rhythm of crickets chirping. The persistent pain of blisters on the soles of our feet tests our patience. Feeling foolish to have refused sandals from the teacher at the temple town, we silently vow to accept the next offer.

A rumbling engine echoes in the distance, its vibration sending tremors up our legs. The noise becomes louder as the headlight of an approaching motorcycle cuts through the darkness. We sidestep the motorcycle as it stops directly in front of us, revealing the figure of a stout man with short curls of hair poking out from a baseball cap. "Hey man, what are you doing out here at this time of night?" he asks.

"Walking."

He smacks his fingertips on his forehead, wiping the perspiration from his eyes. "Do you have somewhere to stay?"

"We have no money to pay for a hotel. We will sleep where we are accepted."

"The next town is many kilometers from here. It is dangerous to travel this road by foot at night . . ." He scratches his head. "Which country are you from?"

We roll our eyes at a familiar question. Sensing our irritation, he says, "Don't be offended, man! The questions are to understand your situation. You seem like you are in need of help. What are your needs?"

"Food in our mouth and a roof over our head."

"See that hotel over there?" He turns, pointing over his shoulder at a large white building standing at the edge of a nearby cliff. "That is my hotel. It has been open for eight days. Go there and sit at one of the tables at the restaurant. The men standing outside will take care of you. Tell them

that you are waiting for Bangari. That is me. I am
going to pick up some medicine in town. We will
talk soon." He grips and twists the handlebars of the
motorcycle, its wheels kicking up dust as it sputters
around the bend.

With the light shining from the hotel as our
guide, we carefully follow a wide curve in the road.
After reaching the hotel, we slide a chair out from
the nearest table and sit down. A young man appears,
carrying a tray. He removes a glass of water from the
tray and places it on the table in front of us.

The trumpet of the motorcycle's engine
heralds Bangari's return. We shield our eyes from
its approaching headlight. Bangari coasts within
arm's length of our table, lowers the motorcycle's
kickstand, turns off its engine, and hops off its seat.
He struts a few paces and then motions to the chair
across from us, awaiting our approval. We nod, and
he pulls out the chair, spreading his arms wide and
landing with a thud. Removing his cap, he tosses it
onto the table and looks at us with intensity. "You
are a madman, to be wandering the Himalayas
without money or a place to go."

"We might not have met you, had we such
things."

"My friend, have you lost your mind?"
Bangari frowns.

"You might say so. But to enter the heart, one must first travel out of the mind. The heart knows the answers to questions the mind can only ponder."

His stern exterior falls away, his eyes softening as he cracks a grin. "Where you come from, or whether you have money, are not important. You are human, and deserve as much as anyone else. You will stay in my hotel tonight, so that you can start fresh tomorrow. These men will feed you and show you to your room." He looks away momentarily, seemingly lost in thought. "Would you mind if we ate together?"

"We prefer together to alone."

Heartened, Bangari confidently raises his hand, shouting in the direction of the kitchen. The waiter returns with his tray, this time carrying two plates with both rice and lentils, and another containing a stack of chapatis. He places the plates on the table, turns and disappears into the kitchen once more. Bangari hunches over his plate, clawing at the food and cramming it into his mouth like a hungry bear. He mumbles between mouthfuls, "What is wrong man, aren't you hungry?"

We laugh. "Of course, only we are used to pecking like the birds."

"Had I known that, I would have offered you some seeds and berries!"

As we eat, a handful of men wander in from out of the darkness, smoking bidis and carrying bottles of wine. Their mood is somber, fatigue showing on their faces as they sit down at one of the tables. Whenever a vehicle approaches, they come to life, waving their arms and calling to its passengers. Every so often a vehicle stops, and Bangari gets up to negotiate the price of a room. After they pass by, the men slink back in their chairs.

A man with a shaved head is roaming the street in front of the hotel. Although he appears young and in good health, he walks with a limp, dragging his left leg behind him. "Don't worry about him, he is my friend," Bangari says. "His name is Ganesh." He points in the direction of a shack next to the hotel. "He lives over there. The government pays him to watch over these barrels in front of my hotel."

Next to the restaurant, a large pit in the ground contains several rows of rusted oil barrels, which are empty. Bangari continues, "He used to walk without a limp. One day he woke up and couldn't move one of his legs. Nobody knows what happened. Not even his wife . . . Now he spends much of the day sleeping, wandering the streets at night. Like you!"

The other men are laughing at Ganesh, slurring slander in between swigs of wine. A tense energy overtakes him; he averts his eyes and turns his body abruptly to deflect their energy. His expression quickly changes from pleasant to sour as he walks into the shack and shuts the door with haste. We feel empathy for Ganesh, who has given his brothers the power to hurt him.

※❀❀❀❀※

Like Ganesh, your Nature determines that you will at times attract negative vibrations, absorbing them into your body. All negative energy is grounded in fear. When you absorb fear-based vibrations, they can burrow into your body like a parasite entering a host. This creates a blockage of energy.

An energy blockage manifests in the physical body as an ailment. This may be a hunch in the shoulders, a convulsing hand, or a twitching face. Mentally, a blockage manifests as negative thoughts and emotions, including frustration, anger, and despair. Spiritually, this creates a locked door that prevents positive states emerging from love, such as peace and happiness. Whenever you block such positive states of being, you deny yourself a fulfilling experience on your Earth walk.

Ganesh is carrying an energy blockage that began as a negative vibration. The blockage is manifesting physically as a limping leg. Mentally, the negative thoughts and emotions that maintain his condition confine him to a shack, where he has limited interactions with his relatives. Spiritually, Ganesh has chosen to ignore those positive states that would allow for healing to take place.

Love has the power to withstand all negativity, be it mental, physical, or spiritual. While steeped in love, you are invulnerable to dis-ease. At the moment of birth, you are immersed in love. This not only protects you, but also enables you to grow and learn at your full potential. You are flexible in your range of movement, having no energy blockages to limit you. Even infants perceived to be sick or handicapped are free from dis-ease, since they arrive in a state that knows nothing of limitation. All children experience a state of ease that is of the highest purity; each pulse from their energy sphere is a joy to behold.

Regardless of your age, you will become rigid if you allow negative energy to accumulate in your body. Whenever your body isn't completely relaxed, your spirit is communicating the presence of negativity. Tension is resistance to the body's natural movements. By learning to recognize tense

areas in your body, you will more effectively be able
to remove the negativity that is responsible for your
suffering.

Fear is the feeling of tension inside that
clutches firmly to negativity. You can detect the
presence of fear from within by becoming aware of
your patterns of breathing. Fear is a forceful gasp of
air, followed by a rapid release. Uneven breathing
creates tension, since it is a form of resistance.
Slow, steady breaths, on the other hand, allow you
to fully experience that state of love which flows
uninterrupted from your being.

You must first acknowledge the presence of
fear before you can open your heart to the possibility
of transformation through love. Recognizing and
taking responsibility for fear can seem challenging.
The moment you are able to admit your own
suffering, you can begin the process of releasing fear.

Rather than tensing in reaction to
negativity, try welcoming its presence, seeing it
as an opportunity to recognize the many faces of
fear. Whenever you absorb negative energy, the
choice exists to try and understand its origins. This
can begin with a question, such as the following:
which habits of thinking might be supporting this
vibration? If the desire exists to change the vibration,
seek to accept the experience into your being. By

accepting the presence of negativity as a part of yourself, you can learn to acknowledge it without holding onto the dis-ease it carries.

Were Ganesh unaffected by his brothers, he would feel no need to shelter his body from the energy that they transmit. He would instead face it directly and without fear, breathing steadily to allow the negativity it carries to pass through him without leaving a trace. By changing the outcome of the encounter, Ganesh would succeed in changing his vibration. Like a parasite without a receptive host, the negativity would continue on without him. This would in turn change the response of the Universe, allowing him new experiences from which to grow and learn. With each new experience, Ganesh would then have the opportunity to absorb positive vibrations with the power to heal his body, mind, and spirit.

❦

A light bulb flickers from inside the shack. During each flash, the outline of Ganesh becomes visible, his nose pressed against the window while he peers in our direction. The image reminds us of the human spirit, destined on one bright morning to abandon its limp as it strides through the doorway with ease.

19

Breath Is the Key

To inhale is to listen to the Universe.
To exhale is to sing in harmony with the Universe.
The space between breaths sustains its melody.

We awaken to the sound of Bangari's voice as the shades are drawn open. "Try on these sandals." He points to an unused pair of sandals lying on the floor beside the bed. The sandals are made of black leather, with two straps across the top and another behind the heel. We slip them onto our feet, fastening their straps. They are a comfortable fit. Bangari squints and nods his head. "Take them. I have plenty of shoes to wear."

He begins pacing across the room, his brow wrinkled with concern. "You are about to enter a jungle that is the home of many large animals. The bears in these parts are known to tear the limbs from men for sport. While we were eating last night, a jaguar passed behind you—a sleek, powerful cat camouflaged by her fur. If she had been hungry, you might have become her prey. You should take my machete, to protect yourself!" He reaches behind his back, removing a leather sheath holding a machete from his belt and laying it on the bed in front of us.

We let out a wide grin, amused by Bangari's dramatic disposition. "We do not fear the jaguar—she is both our friend and a source of great strength. Many fear her power, and it is for this reason she is known to devour them without mercy. We will match her flare, extending our light to the furthest reaches of her being. Love will be our protection."

Bangari throws his hands in the air, sighing as he lowers them. "There is no reason for me to pretend to understand your ways."

"Whenever we accept what we can't understand, we rise above the walls of rejection. If we have done nothing more than open your heart to the power of love, together we will have grown closer to the Truth."

"Your words confuse me, but your heart—that I can relate to." He motions to his motorcycle. "Today I go to visit my family. They live five kilometers north of here. Let me take you at least that far." Before we can object, Bangari picks up our bag and slings it over his shoulder, laughing while he sprints outside in the direction of his motorcycle. He hops on its seat and revs its engine, turning and smirking at us victoriously. Like a younger brother who's been tricked by his sibling, we run to catch up, sheepishly swinging our leg over the seat and then reaching behind us to grip the taillight as the motorcycle speeds off.

At a fork in the road, the motorcycle comes to a stop. Bangari turns to look at us. "Babas always take the road on the right. It will lead you to many different temples." We get off the motorcycle, hug him, and then shake his hand. "Come back down this way," he continues. "Your room will be waiting for you."

We begin walking to the right. Behind us, the motorcycle's engine comes to life, faltering only moments later. "Be careful, my friend!" Bangari's words echo in the distance. "There are wicked people out there who wish evil on foreigners."

"We sympathize with them," we call over our shoulder, "for they are that part of us that has mistaken its reflection for an enemy."

The morning passes quickly while we make our way through the jungle, its thick, verdant foliage at times almost swallowing the road before us. The piercing clicks and chirps of exotic birds fill the air, interrupted only by the occasional purr of a large cat lounging in the shadows. While roaming through the wilderness, the absence of people haunts our conscience. Exactly why the human race left Earth's plentiful refuge to dream up a separate reality remains a mystery. By creating urban landscapes without a hint of her influence, humans have all but forgotten their roots.

Civilization creeps back into our dream as a car buzzes past us. The road begins to widen, the forest retreating behind a series of enormous electrical towers whose power lines reach over several mountaintops. Beneath one of the towers, a tall, frail baba wrapped in a royal purple shawl is seated on a bench beside two *sadhvis*, or female babas. The presence of the sadhvis is a refreshing act of defiance, in a culture that has repressed the feminine pathway for centuries. Oddly enough, in these parts merely associating with females in public is an offense worthy of ridicule. But when you are already an outcast, what is there to lose?

Distracted by the brilliance of the sadhvis' energy spheres, we stumble over a stone person at our feet. A baba from a passing group laughs loudly while we catch our footing, making no attempt to hide his glee. Royal baba frowns, raising his staff and scolding him. The baba cowers in response, lowering his head while passing.

Royal baba stands up, tilting his head in greeting. He bluntly points his staff across the road toward a patch of shrubby plants. "Shortcut." He quickly crosses the street and then steps between the plants, disappearing into the forest. His companions hastily gather their belongings and follow him. Though fatigued, we do not hesitate to follow close behind. Babas with knowledge of the secret trails of antiquity are respected as leaders, since they spare others from the dangers of walking along narrow roads frequented by speeding vehicles.

The trail climbs quickly, the forest canopy shielding us from the sun's intensity. Each breath becomes easier as the leaves of plants and trees brush lightly against our skin. An endless path of large, flat stone people embedded in the ground at our feet reveal the thoughtful gesture of generations of babas pausing to point the way. We broaden our vision, absorbing the browns and greens of Earth's children. From the corner of our eye, a robust antelope skips downhill, the crunch of leaves and twigs the only sound it makes as its hooves rise and fall against the forest floor.

The pavement of a crowded city street suddenly replaces the spongy grass of the forest.

Startled by the commotion, we watch in awe as our companions casually walk in between moving vehicles passing from both directions. Drivers honk and swerve without braking, annoyed yet undaunted by the interruption. At the first lull in traffic we dash across the street, our eyes fixed on royal baba's shawl.

We arrive at an ashram at the outskirts of the city. A group of nearby babas is seated in a circle under a veranda. With eyes closed, they are chanting mantras in unison in a deep, serious tone. Royal baba turns and smiles, waving his staff back and forth in the direction of a large doorway atop a stairwell. He then strolls to the shade of a maple tree, sitting with his back against its trunk. After ascending the stairwell, we enter the open doorway.

Inside, the sight of a handful of babas lying down to rest appeals to our aching body. We fold our blanket, laying it on the cement floor near the wall. The buzzing flies are relentless, even when countered from above by the rotating blades of fans.

A baba in the corner of the room is fiddling with the dial on a radio. Each time he finds a station, he puts it on the floor, and babas begin to hum and sing along with the music. Moments later he grabs the radio, sending waves of static bouncing across the walls as he turns the dial with determination.

Another baba with white hair and beard
is sitting against the wall opposite us. His body is
tense, with skeleton gray eyes lowered to the floor to
avert our gaze. His thoughts float across the room,
entering our awareness soon after we grant their
plea to be heard: *A ritual repeated without feeling will
quickly lose its meaning. Rely on the words and rituals
of others for salvation, and you will end up cold and
broken, like me.* We reflect on his message, careful
not to absorb its defeated vibration.

The figure of a tall, lean baba crosses the
threshold of the doorway with a bold stride. His left
arm ends in a stump just above his elbow, and the
hand of his right arm is missing all but the ring and
index finger. Still, he moves as if blessed, his energy
sphere radiating a green glow. We glance at a nearby
baba, who bows his head reverently and points
toward his relative. His silent message echoes from
within: *Pay attention—there is much to learn from him.*

Blessed baba walks with grace as he
approaches, motioning beside us inquisitively. After
we move our bag to make room, he lays out his
blanket and sits down facing the wall. Lowering his
bag from his shoulder, he holds it open with one
foot, using the other to sort through its contents.
His eyes light up as he discovers the object of
interest. He grabs hold of a smaller bag with both

feet and drops it in front of him. Using the toes of
his foot as one would fingers on a hand, he grasps
a pipe and removes it from the bag. He then uses
the two fingers of his right hand to scrape several
pinches of dried plant medicine into the bowl of the
pipe. He lifts the pipe to his mouth with his foot
and casually looks from side to side.

Several moments pass, the drone of static the
only sound in the room. All of the other babas are
seated motionless, wide-eyed with wonder. Noticing
their expressions, blessed baba laughs. The babas
suddenly break from their trance, talking quickly and
pointing in his direction.

A nearby baba pulls a box of matches from
his pocket. Removing a match, he strikes it against
the box and lowers it to blessed baba's pipe. Blessed
baba puffs the pipe, and the babas return to their
activities.

A group of babas wrapped in shawls are
seated in siddhasana facing the wall, their eyes closed
in meditation. Every so often they half turn their
heads in the direction of radio baba, flashing irritated
expressions.

One of the meditating babas is seated facing
the other babas in the room, with his palms resting
on his knees. He is smiling peacefully despite the
surrounding activity, seemingly absorbed in a state

of bliss. His state of ease is unspoiled by the spiders and other creepy crawlers scuttling across his legs. Blissful baba makes no attempt to hide the tears of joy falling from his eyes.

❦

To meditate is to focus the awareness on an aspect of the present in order to create stillness of mind. Whenever your mind is still, your heart is open to the experience of your unlimited Nature. This experience can liberate you from the reality of a struggling self. Using your eyes to observe an object of Nature is a form of meditation. Closed-eye meditations draw the senses inward to the activity of the body, mind, and spirit. The practice of closed-eye meditation helps the seeker to absorb the calm medicine that accompanies being.

If you wish to practice closed-eye meditation, begin by sitting or lying in any position that feels natural. Close the two eyes at either side of your nose. Breathe steadily, with the same intensity and duration for both the inhalation and the exhalation. Fix your awareness on your breath, finding a rhythm that is comfortable. Thoughts will emerge as your mind fights for control. Still them with your will, for they are obstacles to the state of ease that you seek.

When you are able to achieve a state of relaxation, shift the focus to your heart. Imagine it contained within a closed flower bud—a white rose that, when given enough light, will open its petals in full bloom. Suppose that each petal on the rose is a layer of mind. When the petals are held firmly in place by thoughts, the rose is dormant. If, however, you are able to loosen the grip of your mind on its thoughts, the rose will come to life.

If you focus all of your awareness on opening the rose, as it begins to open, you will feel surges of light travel from your heart to the rest of your body with great speed. This will feel invigorating, like a bolt of lightning moving from the crown of your head down to your hands and feet. These movements of energy are wholesome for your body, mind, and spirit.

The light bursting from your heart as it opens will remind you of the Truth of your connection to creation. At first it may take much focus to open your heart. With practice, the feeling will become natural. Each time you feel the rose petals opening, try to lose yourself in the sensation.

When your heart is completely open, your mind is empty, and the rose petals part to reveal a flower in full bloom. A flourishing flower surrounding the heart reveals a mind stripped of boundaries, and is accompanied by the state of ease.

The more you travel beyond your mind and enter your heart, the easier it will be for you to understand the awareness of blissful baba. The state of ease is like the feeling of relaxation that washes over you as you enter a warm bath, stabilizing your body, mind, and spirit. Whenever your energy sphere is stable, you vibrate a steady wave of love throughout the Universe.

A bell is ringing. Babas instinctively reach for kamandals as the smell of rice pudding drifts in from outside. Catching a glimpse of royal baba's shawl, we rise without thinking. Shortcut.

20

The Light and Dark Principle

A soldier retreats in fear; a sage embraces in love.
Embrace your opposition, and the battle is forgotten.

After a hearty lunch, most of the babas are taking a nap in the shade outside. Feeling energized, we decide to leave the ashram and continue north. Blessed baba winks at us as we bid him farewell.

We walk for much of the afternoon, the sun's heat minimized by a strong wind blowing from the east. Near a town clinging to a ravine, the road splits into several trails leading to a river below. Veering from the road, we follow a dirt path to meditate in solitude at the river's edge.

Near the river, two babas are slouched over a bench. They are wearing long, black garments

symbolic of the tantric tradition. Beside them under
a banyan tree, two men are engaged in a heated
argument. They are gesturing aggressively with their
arms, pointing at one another in accusation. One
is a baba who is wearing a black loincloth, cursing
with rage at a well-dressed young man. The man is
restraining the baba.

Raging baba's expression suddenly changes
from sour to friendly, and he begins hugging the
man and shaking his hand. With splinters of
confusion ruffling his energy sphere, the man turns
and hurries up the ravine.

We feel the impulse to turn and vanish
into the surrounding wilderness. As if sensing our
discomfort, raging baba quickly turns. Noticing us,
he begins walking in our direction, swinging his
arms with exaggeration. It is clear from his glazed
expression and clumsy movements that the spirit of
fire-water has entered his body. Many more spirits
are present, slithering through the shadows behind
his dark eyes.

He stops within arm's reach, his eyelids
drooping as he wipes the saliva from his mouth.
"Why are you here?"

"To meditate near the river."

"If you want to stay here, you must make
me a present of two thousand rupees." He smiles,

revealing a handful of cracked yellow teeth.

"If we had money, we would gladly give it to you. But we don't."

Annoyed, he continues, "You cannot leave here until you make me a present. How about this blanket on your shoulder?" He spits as he talks, his hot, foul breath testing our patience.

"We need our blanket to keep us warm through the night."

He turns to his companions, talking to them heatedly in Hindi. Dissatisfied with their curt replies, he walks within inches of us, spits on our chest, and then strokes our beard with his hand. Lifting his chin with pride, he turns and coils his body into a battle stance, raising his arms in the air and pointing to himself. "Naga baba!" He shoves us backward several paces and then turns his head to peer at us sideways.

We step back and out of his reach, raising our palms. "*Shanti, dost.*" (Peace, friend.) He moves forward, shoving us again as though determined to fight. Encouraged by the laughter of his companions, he winds up and punches our stomach. Although the pain is minimal, our frustration begins to build.

It appears that raging baba has aligned his heart with destructive spirits that are influencing his thoughts and actions. Straining to find traces of emotion in his eyes, we consider reacting with force. But to violently engage with our brother would only allow the negative energy to spread, infecting us as well.

A short, wrinkled baba wearing large, round spectacles appears from a nearby trailhead, wielding a cane. Raging baba is suddenly distracted by his companions, who are cackling like a murder of crows vying for a meal. Soon after we begin walking in the direction of the trailhead, raging baba snaps from his stupor, staggering closer from behind. Before he has the chance to catch us, wrinkled baba confronts him, swinging his cane and scolding him passionately. He turns and winks at us in between shouts, motioning up the ravine. Like our brother before us, we turn and walk briskly away.

After climbing out from the ravine, we are relieved by the change of scenery. No sooner do we escape the chaos below than hysterical laughter breaks out from a nearby tree, echoing throughout the dense jungle canopy. Disguised by the tree's foliage, a gray monkey with a black face hugs its trunk, bobbing its head up and down as it shrieks with laughter.

Amidst the monkey's laughter, the double door of a nearby school swings open, and a herd

of uniformed schoolchildren parade into the street.
They immediately surround us, first pointing, then
sneering, and finally erupting into fits of laughter.
Their cruelty is reflected by the apathy of older
relatives seated on an adjacent bench. The entire
town seems to be consumed by a dark energy similar
to that of raging baba.

❦

If you wish to understand darkness, you
must consider its relationship to light. Before spirit
stitched its robe, it first revealed the dark principle
by imagining a tear in the fabric of light. The
contrast thus created became the foundation of life.
An interpretation of the Truth always begins as
a sacred agreement between light and darkness to
coexist. The interpretation combines the two into a
unique relationship that is expressed by the body.

The light principle includes all positive
states of being that stem from love, while the dark
principle represents all negative states with their
origins in fear. Think of a body as the combination
of physical, mental, and spiritual states of being.
Now imagine your body stripped of its features,
with an outline that is filled in with varying shades
of white and black. The two colors are swirling
together in response to changes in your state of

being; each state reveals a specific combination of light and dark principles.

When a body favors the light principle, loving states of being prevail over fearful states, creating a state of ease. The closer the combination is to pure light, the more stable the state of ease experienced. On the other hand, a body that favors the dark principle will lean toward fearful states of being, which encourage states of dis-ease. Again, the degree of suffering depends on the amount of darkness contained within the body.

Each interaction you have with your relatives involves an exchange of vibrations. As extensions of the body, all vibrations also contain a combination of light and darkness. Each vibration will either pass through, or be deflected by the bodies it encounters. The effect a vibration has on a body depends on how well its combination of light and dark principles matches that of the body.

Deflection occurs when the approaching vibration is denied a point of entry. If a positive vibration in the form of a kind word approaches a body ruled by darkness, the body will deflect the vibration and hence be unaffected. In the same way, a light-prevailing body would deflect a negative vibration in the form of an insult.

A body whose combination of light and darkness is similar to that of an incoming vibration is a receptive vessel to its impact. For example, when a body has chosen the condition of dis-ease by participating in negative states of being, it becomes vulnerable to the cruelty of its relatives. Not only will the body be more likely to absorb negative vibrations, it will also deflect those positive states that would allow for their removal.

All states of being originate within your body. In addition, you are responsible for the vibrations you absorb into your body. For instance, whenever you feel hurt or upset, these emotions will attract similar negative vibrations, which you then have the choice whether to absorb. Were you to place blame on your relatives for the effect of their words and actions, you would be ignoring the negativity that you already possess. This would prolong its presence within your body, which would in turn worsen the consequences.

Once you accept the reality that darkness is always at your side, you can learn to eliminate the suffering it creates by more closely aligning with light. Taking responsibility for the dark principle in your body helps you to recognize its appearance during interactions with your relatives. Once it is recognized, you can apply your will to shift the balance toward a more positive, light-bearing combination.

✳

Thick clouds carried by western winds creep closer. The ground trembles as thunder beings boom across mountains, calling to the lightning clan to herald the rain. Remembering the monkey in the tree, we smile in acceptance of the darkness moving upon us.

21

The Dream of the Heart

Trust the feeling within that knows without thinking.

ain clouds lounge between mountain peaks, spreading their fingers to tickle the trees. An ashram peers through the clouds like a fortress, with red and orange flags hanging from towers standing tall at its four corners. We set our sights in its direction, moving quickly to escape the approaching storm. A large cloud passes through our body, its mist blurring our vision. Beside the ashram's gate, a baba is washing his garments in a stream. Solemn and weary, he ignores our greeting.

We open the gate and follow a walkway lined with whitewashed cement rooms. The rooms' doors are locked, and the shades on their windows are drawn. In front of one of the rooms, a mustached gentleman with a delicate frame sits on a wooden stool with one leg over the other, his head buried in a newspaper. He shoots a disinterested glance in our direction, promptly returning to the paper.

Farther down the walkway, a low wall revealing a grassy field below replaces the rooms to our left. At the opposite end of the field there is a large room with its doors propped open. Several pairs of sandals lie neatly beside its entrance. Many babas are hurrying into the room to escape the rain. We descend a nearby stairwell to the open field, following close behind the babas.

As soon as we reach the doorway, a baba next to us raises his hand, gesturing for us to leave. A neighboring baba begins speaking to him in reassuring tones. Another baba joins the conversation, moving his finger as if to trace a map and then pointing to us. "Baba." His eyes grow wide with intensity when he makes the declaration. We suddenly recognize the faces of many babas met along our journey.

From a dimly lit corner of the room, pleasant baba jumps to his feet and swings his arm around our shoulder, pulling us inside. Rejecting baba bows his head in apology and then motions into the room.

Inside, a group of babas are yelling and pointing in the direction of a woman huddled against

the opposite wall, her arms wrapped around her
legs. Her appearance is disheveled, her clothing dirty
and torn. The babas' tone is condemning, as if the
woman has somehow acted against them. Each time
they accuse her, she replies with a short, high-pitched
shriek, followed by a moan. The babas are persistent,
their voices growing louder in opposition. She
squirms in her seat, bouncing her forehead against her
arms while she jerks her head back and forth.

We soften our vision, dimming our mind
to examine the flow of energy moving throughout
the room. The blood red waves radiating from the
babas are stabbing the air like jagged knives. Though
directed at the woman, the waves interact with
everyone present. Many of the babas are engulfed
by the anger they carry. The woman's energy sphere
is shaded with hues of indigo streaked with scarlet.
She also seems to have absorbed some of the babas'
anger. A small number of babas sit in meditation,
undisturbed by the display. Their spheres are pulsing
with a golden green glow.

The woman stops shrieking. With a raspy
voice, she begins to utter accented syllables, like a
snake spitting venom. Each word seems to reveal
a different language of unknown origin. The babas
fall silent, mystified. We read the energy behind the
words to try and decipher their message. While

envisioning the colors the words suggest, we focus on the sensations their sounds make when they pass through our body. At times her message appears violet, and her tone feels somber. Every so often, a brilliant turquoise outshines the violet, like a ray of hope flitting across the room. The vibrations arouse sympathy from deep within our breast. The woman's words trail off, and she begins to sob. She shivers as she cries. The babas turn their backs in disgust to ignore her.

The dinner bell rings. Grabbing their kamandals, the babas rush out the door. We remain behind, seated against the wall opposite the woman.

Our sister is carrying a dis-ease created by fear. She is holding firmly to negative emotions that are overwhelming her body, mind, and spirit. The emotions have manifested as spirits possessing her body. They are speaking through her, causing her to twitch and moan while she struggles to regain control.

In her search for healing, the woman has wandered into a room full of babas. The babas have judged her to be evil, their angry voices drowning out her pleas. They shun her because they are afraid of being corrupted. The babas' fear blinds them to the possibility of compassion, which could help to alleviate her suffering.

An active mind is the sound of many voices engaged in an argument. Each shouts without listening, convinced of its own significance. For every voice of your mind that guides your spirit on its chosen path, ten more mislead by spreading doubts and confusion. Your task is to sort through the voices, deciding which to favor.

When the voices of your mind allow your emotions free rein, your body and spirit can become vulnerable to their influences. Intense emotions behave like a powerful magnet, attracting matching vibrations. The more intense the emotion you experience, the more likely you are to absorb similar vibrations.

When the woman at the ashram listens to those voices that promote feelings of despair, she attracts similar negativity from her relatives. The angry, condemning babas are physical manifestations of the fears she entertains in her mind. Similarly, the negative spirits she has welcomed into her body are the spiritual manifestation of the same fears. When she again chooses to favor positive voices, her vibration will change, along with her experience.

The practice of listening cultivates an awareness of the many voices of your mind. When you journey inward through meditation, you develop your ability to better hear and understand the details of your dream. This dream begins in your heart, quickly expanding to surround your body's energy sphere. Your heart acts as the control center, choosing the content of your dream to be either simple or complex, happy or sad, loving or fearful. The choices you make determine the Nature of your experience.

Dreams are like the branches of a tree, forever reaching toward the light. As they compete with one another, some are shaded by the leaves of their siblings. The tree will cast off smaller, weaker branches that prevent its growth, allowing its strongest branches to receive the most light. In this way, the tree grows tall and beautiful.

There exists a voice in each of us that never strays from the dream of the heart. When the heart is steeped in love, this voice becomes the tallest branch on the tree, in full view of the light. Follow its lead, and you will become illumined from within. Ignore the voice of love, and you will stumble through the darkness created by fear.

Each time you inhale, you have a choice. You can exhale a loving vibration that supports the state of ease, or a fearful vibration that supports the state of dis-ease. Cruel words and gestures are fearful vibrations that disrupt harmony. These vibrations carry a destructive power that can harm both the giver and receiver. The awareness of fear spreads dis-ease by severing the connection between relatives.

Kind words and gestures, on the other hand, create loving vibrations that have a positive impact on our relatives. Such vibrations possess a healing power that can benefit both the giver and receiver. This is because the awareness of love recognizes the receiver as an extension of the giver.

❦❦❦

We imprint a vibration into a nearby blanket; a prayer from our heart, written in a language her spirit will understand. The prayer reads: *Lift this woman from the depths of fear unharmed.* Rising and carrying the blanket across the room, we place it at her feet. With tears in her eyes, she looks away in shame, no longer able to conceal a turquoise wave flooding her heart.

22

The Space of Separation

*The furrowed brow of a mind absorbed in thought will
keep the Truth locked away within the heart.
Open your heart and feel the color
overflow the spaces of your mind.*

"Hari om. Hari om." An early-bird baba's praises
to the Universe echo throughout the room.
We blink our eyes open to the grunts and sighs of
babas yawning and stretching, coughing and spitting.
A baba pats his belly and says, "Chai," during a
conversation with himself. Outside, more babas
bathe beneath a waterfall, shivering while brushing
their teeth and combing their beards and hair.
Others squat by the water, clutching bars of soap
as they scrub their clothes against flat stone people.
"Chai." A baba smacks his lips and glances from side

to side with mischief in his eyes. Babas sit patiently, removing tin cups from kamandals. "Chai." Babas check their watches, fold blankets and tie bundles. *Chai.* A steady mantra gaining momentum. Babas wait anxiously, already walking within their minds.

A man enters carrying a large tin bucket. The babas huddle around him, holding out their cups like anxious children. He removes a ladle and begins serving. After receiving the steaming, fragrant liquid, we sit with the other babas in a circle, passing crackers amidst a chorus of dipping and chewing and sipping. Gratitude: the awareness that can find contentment in a cup of tea.

We descend a stairwell to the empty street below, a line of babas in tow. The line spills into the street like a puddle, splitting into groups of threes and fours. Using the cool morning to our advantage, we walk without stopping, declining our brothers' invitations to join them for a smoke. Our brisk pace whisks us from the pack and into the solitude of the wilderness.

The morning shadows vanish beneath the tread of our footsteps, the heat of the midday sun now baking Earth's skin. Each breath becomes deeper while we climb the shoulder of the mountain. Just as suffering begins to sneak up from behind, the song of a man concealed by a thicket of evergreens permeates our being. We halt in our tracks, gripped by his glorious praises. A vigorous baba rounds the bend in the road ahead, serenading the forest with a celestial melody.

Singsong baba stops abruptly in front of us, his expression playful and innocent. A bulky black bag falls from his shoulders, hitting the ground with a thud. He looks at us through oval eyes with sand-colored centers, pointing downhill and speaking in Hindi. We shake our head in confusion. Realizing our difficulty, he brings his fingers to his mouth. "*Khitchari, aik* kilometer." (Khitchari, one kilometer.) His words invoke the enticing image of rice and lentils bathed in ghee and stained bright yellow with turmeric.

A gathering of hawks soars above, weaving its message across the sky: *Step backward to move forward*. Grinning, singsong baba grabs our arm, leading us downhill.

Together we approach a modest hut grasped by the vining limbs of the forest. A fountain carved from a boulder sits beside its entrance, water pouring from the mouth of a fish into a basin below. Singsong baba removes his sandals and enters the hut, speaking in humble tones to a man inside. A fire cackles while the smell of cooking oil drifts through the doorway.

In the distance, the blurred outline of a young baba appears, his image gathering detail as he draws nearer. He is without a shirt and sandals, with no bag or blankets across his shoulders, and no kamandal in his hand. His strides are as elegant as a swan gliding across a lake. Fine black hair extends below his shoulders, rising and falling with his footsteps like the tail of a prancing horse. With each movement, he seems to carry the landscape with him. The whites of his eyes are majestic, resembling pearls shining from the depths of a bottomless ocean.

Pearl baba approaches just as singsong baba exits the hut. He notices pearl baba and impulsively reaches out his arm to stop him. After motioning to the hut beside us, singsong baba moves his thumb and forefinger to and from his mouth. Pearl baba nods in understanding.

A stout, middle-aged man emerges from the darkness of the hut with his eyes rolled into the back of his head. He holds up an open right palm while walking, bowing with each step as if to praise the ground under his feet. We all follow him to an adjacent canopy made of sticks and burlap, removing our sandals. He motions with open palms for us to sit, then turns and disappears into the hut once again.

More babas enter from the road. Pearl baba sits across from us in siddhasana, with his navel tucked in, his chest heaved out, and his shoulders raised. His movements are slow and subtle, like a silent statue rousing from centuries of stillness. Our eyes meet, his gaze surveying our being and continuing into the depths of infinite. There is a certainty about his expression that exposes our innermost fears and misgivings, as if he is holding a mirror to our heart. Startled, we look down in disbelief, repulsed by the image before us. Ripples of anxiety emanate from our energy sphere. Pearl baba remains fixed in his seat, unmoved by our reaction.

The host returns, carrying a large bowl in his hands. He removes a wooden spoon from the bowl and begins to serve neighboring babas. Hunger pangs sound from within. Still, we do not dare to look up, lest pearl baba reveal our dark principle once again.

How easily we cast our failures onto an innocent guest—as if he were somehow responsible for our thoughts and emotions! In a moment of clarity, the voice of our heart cuts through the confusion: *Why resist this part of you with such hostility?* We suddenly recognize the veil of separation, draped over the mirror as an excuse to cloak our folly.

Pearl baba hasn't spoken a word, hasn't so much as blinked. His manner remains calm, like a spider posted in its web. Although we are able to regard neighboring babas without hesitation, when we glance at pearl baba, disturbance echoes from within. We begin to tremble, like a soldier confronting its enemy. Our apprehension reminds us of Ganesh.

The voice of our heart returns, this time offering an alternative: *Remove the veil. Face your reflection.* Overcoming fear's resistance, we meet the gaze of our friend, controlling the impulse to turn and look away. Our vision softens, stripping the layers of judgment shrouding our connection—those deceptive, destructive patterns of mind that insist on hierarchies to satisfy the self's search for stardom. If we could only remember our collective grandeur, the Truth that will forever remain our only hope for salvation!

❧❧❧

At the moment you are reading these words, you have only just begun to recognize the veil of separation. If you wish to understand your connection to creation, you must first learn how to train your eyes to remove boundaries.

Come to an awareness of your breath, until you are breathing steadily. Allow your mind to become still. When you feel calm, close your eyes, imagining the space around you filled with energy as pure as falling snow. Now open your eyes again, noticing the life that has entered to fill this sacred space. Know that although life appears to you in different forms, their essence is shared.

With your eyes still open, fix your awareness on the rose in your heart, opening it with your will. Visualize a sphere of energy that is the color and purity of lightning surrounding the rose. Focus on expanding this sphere of light until you feel its energy containing your entire body.

As the sphere of white light begins to pulse beyond your body, you will experience an intensified feeling of connection to creation. Your vision will soften, blurring the lines of your mind. When this happens, it is because you are consciously merging your energy sphere with the life that surrounds you. You will notice your awareness become more fluid, like a rolling wave in a vast ocean. Tears may even form in your eyes. Try to remain with this feeling.

Now shift your focus to a nearby life-form. This could be any member of Earth's tribe. As you observe the form in front of you, allow all that is in the background to fade. Next, allow the boundary of the life-form to blur. If you focus on the space just beyond the outline, you will begin to see a faintly colored sphere pulsing from its body. The color of the sphere is related to the emotions of the life-form. The more its boundary blurs, the more brilliant the colors radiating from its body will appear to you.

When the space of separation is completely removed, you will notice the life-form's energy sphere expanding in waves of color that fill the landscape. At this moment, if you consciously expand your sphere to merge with that of your reflection, its experience will be yours to share.

❀❀❀

Pearl baba finishes his meal, rising from his seat. He then turns and walks back to the road, his image becoming more of the scenery with each stride as he continues downhill. Content to share the light that considers all of creation its favorite, we bow in reverence for the sage that is everywhere at once.

Singsong baba taps our shoulder, rubbing his palm against a clean plate. Taking his cue, we scrub our dish with a handful of dirt and rinse it in the fountain's basin. After returning the dish to our host with gratitude, we join the company of

singsong baba and friends, entering the road and
continuing north.

Before long, singsong baba has convinced all
of us to learn his contagious melody. Together our
voices soar up and over mountaintops. Windows
and doors open at each passing town, their
inhabitants absorbing our playful wave. What began
as a small group quickly grows to a gathering, with
babas and townspeople alike joining the chorus.

Two adolescent boys step out from the
shadows of a nearby alley and into the flock. Their
tattered clothes and dirt-smeared faces serve as
evidence of the trials endured, arousing feelings
of kinship amongst the babas. We pretend not to
notice while the boys sneak their way to safety at
the center of the group. Many babas are smiling to
nobody in particular, remembering former selves:
rebellious runaways, drifting at the margins of a
society with which they disagree. A society that
regards Mother Earth as an outcast to be banished
behind walls built with fear as their foundation; a
stubborn, narrow perspective that will meet its end
today in two children who have had enough.

Together we represent the voices of the
Golden Dawn, inviting our relatives to grow beyond
fears that imprison the spirit. Descending to Earth
with the force of shooting stars, we are summoning

the memory of the Truth to chart our course. Power is our birthright, and we intend to use it to transform the dull stone of suffering into a shining diamond.

We are voyagers sailing across the ocean of existence, grabbing hold of a spinning wheel to steer an ancient course for humankind. Each day our numbers grow, uniting to form a wave carrying the imprint of love; a wave on a collision course with the hearts of our relatives.

23

Communion

The self is a dis-ease, for which Nature offers release.
Nature's promise is salvation, to all creatures in
communion. Communion is the deer in our fields, the
fish in our oceans, and the birds atop our trees. Imagine
a family unbound by numbers or appearance; with no
I left to suffer, it finds eternal nourishment in We.

We reach the end of the road. Next to a crowd of people and vehicles, mules stand patiently in a line at the entrance to a cobblestone trail. Young men clutch the reins, whistling and shouting to entreat travelers on foot to pay for a ride. The trail is steep and narrow, moving quickly uphill and then turning sharply out of sight. Small, lean Nepali elders with large wooden baskets strapped to their backs wince as they carry either an elderly woman or a small child. Every now and again, a group of four men standing two by two stomp past carrying long wooden poles atop their shoulders. Attached to the poles is a throne, on top of which a person is seated. The men shout as they pass, scattering mules and people alike to the fringes of the trail.

The ground is muddy from the endless tread of hooves and feet. Trudging uphill, we struggle to maintain our footing while avoiding traffic from both directions. Our thighs soon begin to burn from battling the merciless terrain. Everyone around us is moving with urgency, their thoughts fixed on reaching the top of the mountain. Amidst the chaos, there is the whir of helicopters piercing the clouds overhead.

After climbing the mountain for much of the morning, the steep trail begins to transition into a gently sloping plateau. Clouds looming near the mountain's summit part briefly, allowing a glimpse of a humble town nestled between snow-capped peaks. The town's numerous walkways converge at a golden temple glistening proudly as its centerpiece.

Near the outskirts of town, a helicopter descends from the clouds, landing on top of a painted cross inside a circular helipad. A family emerges from the helicopter and begins to mirror our stride. Together we cross a short bridge and enter the flow of traffic leading to the temple.

Merchants line the streets, selling prashad, wood carvings, and brass figures of Hindu deities. As we draw closer to the temple, the familiar faces of pleasant baba, pearl baba, and royal baba surface in the crowd; they nod to acknowledge us, joining the procession.

We ascend a short stairwell and step onto a broad platform at the base of the temple. A group of babas sits proudly beneath a nearby stone canopy, smoking and chatting while passersby drop change into open kamandals. Armed military men wearing helmets circle the temple, their heels clicking in cadence while music blares from a loudspeaker above its entrance. An Aghori baba painted in white puffs a chilam, holding his free arm raised and dancing in a frenzy. A nearby baba leans in close. "He hasn't lowered his arm for over a year now, to show his commitment to his faith."

A well-dressed man wraps his arm around our shoulders, his companion aiming her camera and taking a picture. The flash of the camera sends our vision reeling. We pause to look around. Somewhere amidst the activity, we became separated from the other babas.

A young girl wearing a sky-blue hooded robe that matches her eyes approaches, frowning. With fingers interlaced at her waist, she rises on her toes, leaning slightly forward. "Aren't you going inside?"

Before we can answer, a crashing noise resounds through the temple's walls. A hush falls over the crowd as guards muscle their way against the flow of men, women, and children rushing to safety. Whispers circulate from ear to ear, speaking of a man overturning tables inside. The guards resurface and surround the entrance, empty-handed and suspicious.

A wiry, elderly man wearing a pair of spectacles and a loincloth passes by, fanning himself with a handful of peacock feathers. When he passes, he lifts his chin and peers over his spectacles to grin at us. A boy carrying a large clay urn trails several paces behind, water splashing onto the ground as he hurries to keep pace.

While watching the crowd of pilgrims, we recognize a familiar desperation in their eyes. One searches for entertainment, hoping to capture fascinating images that delight the senses on the film of a camera. Another searches for a revelation to relieve the spirit from the battle against itself. Many more seek distraction: an adventure to escape the recurring nightmare their reality has become. All are looking outward, awaiting an answer that seems to beckon from somewhere in the distance — as if the fulfillment of our dreams were brought to us in a stork's mouth, in a future that is yet to arrive. For as long as we feel separate from our relatives, Great Spirit will appear to be a mysterious figure residing in a time outside of now.

The platform at our feet suddenly transforms into a transparent rainbow, a portal beneath which the muddy ground can be seen. A pair of white swans materializes from the rainbow; beating their wings gracefully, they guide an ivory chariot with eagle plumes for wheels. Gripping the chariot's reins is a tall, genderless figure resembling a human with serpent-yellow eyes, flowing black hair, and cobalt skin. The chariot spirals upward, turning to face us upon reaching the apex of the temple.

The figure begins to shape-shift, rapidly changing from monkey to kitten to crow, like a jester mocking our attempt to explain the infinite. Bewildered, we blink intently to remove this seeming trick of vision. The more we focus on the images before us, the more blurred and deceptive they become, until finally vanishing altogether. After we shift our gaze to a vacant cloud nearby, the form instantly returns, reverting to its human outline. To our dismay, each time we meet its gaze, an invisible power cloaks the display.

Frustrated, we surrender to the elusive Nature of our counterpart. There is a sensation of release, and our spirit begins to float up and away from Earth. We watch from above as our body collapses into the forgetfulness of slumber. Before we can drift past the chariot, the figure reaches out and curls its fingers into its palm. The currents carrying our awareness submit to their pull like strings to a puppeteer, boarding the spectral vessel beside our cobalt companion.

Sound replaces form, our awareness impressing upon space like the emblazoned encore of a shooting star. Images dim to darkness; the clock of WoMan unravels amidst motion's sudden departure. After ascending beyond Earth's sonic dreamscape, we expand to fill the emptiness of a boundless void. We have returned to the abode of our ancestors, who are engaged with the creation of all possible worlds at once.

A white spark ignites from the darkness of the Great Mystery, traversing the heart of silence like a spiraling snake. Each revolution creates a lens of light: a window allowing us the opportunity to witness an aspect of existence. Accepting the invitation to merge with our spiral, we behold the Truth from behind a single lens.

Waves of color engulf us as our spirit returns to the labyrinth of form. Blue and green crystallize into the familiar reality of Mother Earth viewed from afar. All colors of the rainbow penetrate our lens while we draw nearer to Earth, harmonizing with her vibration.

We descend in the form of a butterfly into an open meadow dazzled with wildflowers, adorning Earth's skin in splashes of scarlet, violet, and emerald. The buzzing wings of hummingbirds fill the air, pausing to sip the flowers' nectar. A weeping willow stands tall at the meadow's navel, and there is a youthful man seated with eyes closed at its base. He is smiling in blissful reverie, his manner unassuming. We enter a bluebird's nest at the top of the tree, becoming a member of a chirping choir calling to mother for the morning meal.

A woman and child stroll through an orchard in the distance, admiring its trees as they forage for fruit. The woman walks with grace, bending slightly to hold the hand of the excited boy. A basket of apples, figs, and walnuts hangs from her opposite arm. We feel our awareness drift downward like a falling leaf, entering the seated man through the crown of his head. Our eyes open to behold the woman leading the boy to us, her flowing dark curls parting from her face to reveal a sublime countenance. The boy is smiling with radiance, a Buddha expressing a pristine love for creation.

The two approach and sit across from us, the three of us forming a triangle. Language returns to indulge our mind, as a query surfaces from the stillness: *Could Master babaji appear as a beautiful enchantress? Or might the young boy's sparkle betray the Master's trickery?*

The woman's soothing voice breaks the silence. "Which do you believe it ought to be?"

We glance quizzically from the woman to the boy and back again. The young boy laughs cheerfully, as though teasing our severity. "The believer gets the final say!" He motions to our heart, his belly lurching while he giggles energetically. Blushing, we are once again reminded of the wisdom of innocence.

Sensing our embarrassment, the woman hushes the boy with a wave of her hand. She strokes his hair with tenderness, removing a stubborn lock from his eyes and tucking it over his ear. "Precious child, a kind and patient manner is more insightful than a lifetime of sarcasm." He bows his head bashfully, glancing at her from the corner of his eye. She places her basket within his reach. "Here, why don't you have some fruit?" The boy sorts through its contents, removing a handful of figs. He tosses one into his mouth and begins chewing hungrily.

Seeing her son occupied, the woman turns back to us. "Now, a question for you. If we were to believe that *you* are Master babaji, who would have the right to tell us otherwise?" We hesitate, confused.

She continues, "Hold your peace—listen closely. If Master babaji approached as a sick woman, would you attend to her health? Or if he swam as a dolphin, would you keep his oceans fresh? What if it was the air in your lungs—would you savor each breath? To see the Master as one among the many, this is life's ultimate test."

"To answer a question with many more seems to only further the mystery!" The words spill from our mouth.

She smiles, amused by our outburst. "The Universe is magic. Its answers are questions."

The young boy turns his head, distracted by a rustle from close behind. Gazing past him, we notice a spotted doe resting in the shade at the margin of the forest, ears perked in the direction of three fawns rolling in the tall grass. A bear cub with a mouthful of berries splashes playfully in a nearby creek. The boy shrieks with delight, clapping his hands and bouncing where he sits.

Instinctively reaching out our arms, we fold our hands in theirs to bridge the space of separation. The absence of thought enhances our embrace. Together we watch as three seemingly separate energy spheres consciously merge, creating a collective sense of wellness.

A congregation of humans manifests from a grove of cedar trees at the forest's edge. Emanations of WoMen and children of all ages and races approach from the four directions. They surround us and sit in an ever-widening spiral, their hands clasped together in an unbroken chain.

The woman looks to us. "Your quest for Master babaji has led you to conjure this vision from the dream. Here you sit at the center of existence, your heart filled with love for creation. The humans surrounding you have followed their hearts' vibrations in search of the Truth, venturing here in spirit to listen to your interpretation of mastery. Speak to them. Accept the reality that you are Master babaji."

A crystal pedestal passes through Earth at the center of the spiral. When we stand to address our audience, we recognize the face of every WoMan and child encountered during our Earth walk. The words flow effortlessly from our being, as though rehearsed many times. "You are already the embodiment of mastery. This realization returns to your awareness whenever you enter the state of

communion, which involves merging with all forms
of existence at once. Communion begins with an
awareness of surrounding life-forms.

"As you sit here in this meadow, notice all
the green life Earth wears on her body, from the lush
plants and soft grass, to the lofty trees and vibrant
flowers. Enjoy the sensations while you pass your
hands through them. Use your intention to direct
the waves of your energy sphere into theirs. Be gentle
and reverent, addressing them like you would an old
friend. Thank them for sharing this moment with
you. Give them the recognition they deserve, and
they will bless you with their wisdom, offering their
interpretation of the Truth. Accept it with humility.

"Follow this sequence in your interactions
with Nature. Swallow your tongue for a moment —
remember the language of your heart. Return to that
blossoming flower inside you that isn't afraid to ask
the turtle why his shell is striped, and doesn't feel
ashamed to praise the beauty of a canary's song at
dusk. Absorb the feeling of expansion as you reflect
on the majesty of the present.

"Approach each experience as an opportunity
to understand the relatedness of life. Look within
your heart for the common ground that removes the
solid outline of the self, replacing it with a seamless
wave of color and sound. This is your refuge — here

you will discover the end of all suffering. Take heart in the rediscovery of one another as close relatives to be honored.

"Whenever you enter into communion with your relatives, your love for them grows stronger. Love is not an obligation, or an act of hard labor, but rather an effortless expression that fills you with joy. If you can welcome this expression into your daily life, it will transform your experience on Earth into one of lasting contentment.

"Love teaches us of a power that is grander in scale than the self. This tremendous power is bestowed at birth, and can never be removed. It begins and ends within your heart. Like the sun, its energy flows without reserve, and it has no need for compensation. Coursing through your veins like a steed of horses, it carries with it the promise of liberation from suffering.

"Each time you feel fear, you block this power. Fear travels deep into the chambers of your heart, building walls around its light — a light that would otherwise shield you from dis-ease. When you allow the destructive forces of fear to enter your heart, you forget the unlimited power bestowed through love.

"Once blocked, this power cannot be bullied into revealing itself. It knows nothing of the material realm, so it carries no price. It will not rouse for prayers repeated without understanding. You can fast, sing and dance, make sacrifices and offerings— you can even climb the tallest mountains to visit the holiest of temples. Still, it will elude you. For as long as fear remains, your connection to the heart's power will remain severed.

"Fortunately, the heart's power has never left your side. The walls were built by the self, and will respond to the right intention. Your will can overcome any obstacle. Take all of the power in the institutions, all the wisdom in the books and return it to its rightful place: your heart. All the secrets of the ancients, all the answers to the Great Mystery lie dormant in the buried treasure within your chest. Love is the key to open the chest.

"Love is acceptance of that rushing steed, that power which is our birthright as living, breathing reflections of Great Spirit. It is the grand prize waiting at the altar. All are invited to reclaim their power—the opportunity is ever present. Stand tall alongside your relatives, together we can break through the walls of fear that cloak the Truth."

We step down from the pedestal, taking our place in the spiral. Our female complement reaches both arms skyward, parting the clouds. She takes hold of first the sun, and next the moon, each appearing as a miniature orb from within her grasp. As she touches them to the crystal at the center of the spiral, a spark ignites inside the heart of every WoMan and child. All are suddenly consumed by the passionate flames of creation, like a phoenix poised for flight.

23 ½

Departure

*A spirit that dreams is like a star moving through
space. As it moves it sends spheres of light, streaming
forth as a wave. The wave strikes as it travels,
all dreams within reach. A planet is a meeting
place, a raindrop in a lake, for stars to reflect on
their dreams, before continuing on their way.*

There exists a place deep within the heart of
WoMan. A beam of light emerging from
the shadows at the end of time depicts a land of
boundless space. Its features are of Earth: her rolling
prairies, stoic mountains, and surging springs. Here
all life-forms are glowing with an inner light finding
no reason for containment. Each robe of spirit
gives and takes harmoniously, forever sustained by
the awareness of unity that allows for plenty. All

tongues are understood, all interpretations accepted and nurtured during their passage.

Humanity will rise again to the role of the steward, to honor the life upon Mother Earth for generations to come. Your heart will determine love to be its only motive, coaxing your mind into admiration for the melody of existence. You will join all members of Earth's tribe to herald the reign of peace. Together you will set your sights upon the horizon to witness the Return of the Golden Dawn, its light transforming the nightmare of suffering into the paradise of communion.

The energy sphere of Earth and her tribe will brighten to reflect the wellness radiating from within. All will be blessed by the gratitude they possess. Here nothing will be lacking, and no answer hidden from view. Humbled by Nature's glorious expression, your adoration will liberate you from the struggles of the self. The tempest will recede, a rainbow appearing in its wake. The burden will fly from your heart to reveal the gift of life everlasting.

Star beings from distant suns have visited Earth since her entry from the fiery womb of her parents. We are your guardians, honoring each of our robed relatives as a sacred translation of light. Liberated from the laws of the body, we float through space like clouds, falling to Earth to cradle her tribe. We are the invisible ones, responding to your heart's alarm by revealing the path to safety. Your vision from above, we are here to guide you through the jungle of fear until you again reach the meadow of love.

Your fate is ours to share—we witness your victories and defeats. Enter the forest with moonlight as your guide; we will appear to you as flashing fireflies, illuminating the shadows in spheres of green, gold, and white. Enter the stillness of your mind with breath as your guide; we will appear to you as sensations of warmth that enter your body and travel up your spine. Our vibration is the heartfelt joy you express while walking in harmony with your relatives.

Our message is clear, should you choose to lend an ear: love is the strongest medicine. Love's power is to remove all suffering through the memory of our connection. All beings in Earth's tribe and beyond are called to realize this awareness. To do so, we must work together to clear all thoughts that sever our connection, giving rise to dis-ease of the body, mind, and spirit. Dis-ease is a chosen condition, conceived by a mind that flinches at its own creation. The heart's love serves as peacemaker, drawing the treatise to reverse the spell. When love aligns our body, mind, and spirit in harmony, we flower into the state of ease.

Children of Earth's tribe, unite! Look now upon the horizon, the dawn is already upon you. With love as your savior, may you remember your light.

Your body is light, to sculpt as you please.
All beings are one, separate though they may seem.
Remember: you are here to reflect on the dream.

Stone-people's house.

Comfortable fit.

Holy Ganges.

Mules resting after a long day.

Suraj sewing outside his tent.

Single file.

Steady footing...

Terraced grainfields.

Bangari insists.

Walk at your own risk.